BEHAVING IN PUBLIC

Behaving in Public

HOW TO DO
CHRISTIAN ETHICS

Nigel Biggar

William B. Eerdmans Publishing Company

Grand Rapids, Michigan / Cambridge, U.K.

Published 2011 by
Wm. B. Eerdmans Publishing Co.
2140 Oak Industrial Drive N.E., Grand Rapids, Michigan 49505 /
P.O. Box 163, Cambridge CB3 9PU U.K.

Printed in the United States of America

17 16 15 14 13 12 11   7 6 5 4 3 2 1

Library of Congress Cataloging-in-Publication Data

Biggar, Nigel.
Behaving in public: how to do Christian ethics / Nigel Biggar.
p.   cm.
Includes bibliographical references (p. m   ) and index.
ISBN 978-0-8028-6400-0 (pbk.: alk. paper)
1. Christian ethics — Anglican authors. 2. Social ethics.
3. Social policy — Moral and ethical aspects.   I. Title.

BJ1251.B49   2011
241 — dc22

2010041869

www.eerdmans.com

To Jim Gustafson,

mentor,

with gratitude

Ma place est parmi les Gentils;

et ma mission . . . de dire ce que je crois vrai

sans demander aucun mot d'ordre, sans engager

personne que moi-même,

en demeurant partout et toujours

ut témoin.

François Mauriac*

*"Le Bloc-notes," *L'Express,* 12 février 1957, in François Mauriac, *Bloc-notes,* ed. Jean Touzot, 5 vols., Vol. 1, "1952-57" (Paris: Seuil, 1993), p. 443: "My place is among the Gentiles, and my mission . . . to say what I believe to be true without demanding any watchword, without enlisting anyone but myself, while remaining always and everywhere a witness." I thank Professor Paul Cooke of the University of Exeter for helping me track down the exact provenance of this quotation.

Contents

Acknowledgments

In writing this book I have received help from several quarters.

First of all, Jon Pott, editor-in-chief at the Wm. B. Eerdmans Publishing Company, put an idea into my mind — during the 2008 meeting of the Society for Christian Ethics — that grew into this book. Then, since the autumn of 2008, Alonzo McDonald and the McDonald Agape Foundation have generously supported my work through the establishment of the McDonald Centre for Theology, Ethics, and Public Life at the University of Oxford.

The original drafts of the first four chapters of *Behaving in Public* comprised the Centre's inaugural series of McDonald Lectures in February 2009. Thanks to the initiative of Dr. John Perry, the new McDonald postdoctoral fellow in Christian Ethics and Public Life, I was able to learn from the reactions of the Oxford postgraduates in Christian ethics who congregated in the Head of the River pub on March 5, 2009: Therese Feiler, Guido de Graaff, Rob Heimburger, Chris Jones, Tom Kirby, and Phil Lorish.

On September 3, the same nascent chapters were the subject of discussion at the annual meeting of the McDonald Centre's Public Discourse Group in the Red Bull pub in Cambridge. Those present were Mark Bratton, Malcolm Brown, Jonathan Chaplin, Neil Messer, Esther Reed, and Robert Song. Christopher Insole was absent, but he sent comments afterward.

On September 22, I was privileged — thanks to the recommendation of Robin Lovin — to deliver an abbreviated version of chapters 1 through 4 as the 2009 Willis M. Tate-Willson Lectures at Southern Methodist University. My SMU colleagues were unstinting in their hospitality. Later in the autumn, Esther Reed commented on the first draft of chapter 5, and Dave Leal and David Clough reviewed a complete draft of the whole book.

To all these friends and colleagues — for their various investments, their candor, and their encouragement — I am enormously grateful.

Certain passages in Chapters 1, 2, 3, and 5 have been drawn, in more or less modified form, from previously published work of mine: *The Hastening That Waits: Karl Barth's Ethics* (Oxford University Press, 1995), pp. 147-51; "Karl Barth and Germain Grisez on the Human Good: An Ecumenical *Rapprochement,*" in *The Revival of Natural Law: Philosophical, Theological, and Ethical Responses to the Finnis-Grisez School,* ed. Nigel Biggar and Rufus Black (Ashgate, 2000), pp. 176-79; "Saving the Secular: The Public Vocation of Moral Theology," *Journal of Religious Ethics* 37.1 (March 2009): 170-72; and "Not Translation, but Conversation: Theology in Public Debate about Euthanasia," in *Religious Voices in Public Places,* ed. Nigel Biggar and Linda Hogan (Oxford University Press, 2009), pp. 166-70, 171-72. This material reappears here with the kind permission of Oxford University Press, Ashgate Publishing, and John Wiley and Sons.

Preface

I dedicate this book to my doctoral supervisor at the University of Chicago, James Gustafson. I have long admired Jim for not making disciples out of his students. If there are any "Gustafsonians" out there, I am not aware of being one. Nevertheless, in the course of writing this book I have become increasingly conscious of the weight of my debt to him. After I had completed a first draft, I read — for the first time since buying it in the early 1980s — *Can Ethics Be Christian?*[1] There I was (pleasantly) surprised to discover Jim's pursuit of a middle course that anticipates my own by thirty-five years.

Then, after bringing *Behaving in Public* to a conclusion by locating its moral theological position in "Barthian Thomism," it dawned on me that it is probably not a coincidence that the very first course in Christian ethics that I ever took was Gustafson's famous seminar comparing the ethics of Thomas Aquinas and Karl Barth, nor that one of the few books of his that I did read as a student was *Protestant and Roman Catholic Ethics: Prospects for Rapprochement.*[2] Finally, it strikes me that in his combination of human and spiritual seriousness, theological convic-

---

1. James M. Gustafson, *Can Ethics Be Christian?* (Chicago: University of Chicago Press, 1975).

2. James M. Gustafson, *Protestant and Roman Catholic Ethics: Prospects for Rapprochement* (Chicago: University of Chicago Press, 1978). Was this book echoing in the depths of my subconscious when, in 2000, I entitled an essay of mine "Karl Barth and Germain Grisez on the Human Good: An Ecumenical *Rapprochement*"? Very probably: "rapprochement" is not a word I use much.

tion ("Say something *theological!*"), and honest engagement with other sciences, Jim has actually embodied much of the model of Christian ethics that I have sought to recommend in these pages. For all these reasons, therefore, it is fitting that I record my gratitude to him here, and I do it gladly.

Introduction

What follows is a view from somewhere.

It was the winter of 1973, and I was in my very first term as an undergraduate reading Modern History at Oxford. Huddled over the desk in my room in the dark morning hours, I was straining to prepare for my first set of exams by candlelight, since the electricity-generating stations had shut down, their fuel supply cut off by striking coalminers. My tea was not sweet, as I preferred, since the dockyard workers were also on strike, and imported sugar was impossible to find. The radio was heavy with news about the latest bombings and shootings in Northern Ireland, where the violence was then at its height. And the London *Times* was running a series of leading articles under the title "Is Britain Governable?" Like everyone else — except perhaps for those on the hard left, who were gleeful about the revolutionary opportunities of economic and political chaos — I was anxious and concerned. And as a recent convert to Christianity, I wondered what on earth my newfound faith had to say to such a national crisis.

Three years later the crisis had passed, but the political strife rumbled on. I was now in the final year of my undergraduate studies and I had opted to take a specialist course on the life and times of Saint Augustine, in which large tracts of *The City of God* (in Latin) were prescribed. Here I found another Christian who was trying to make sense of turbulent times in which the known world seemed to be falling down about his ears. Nothing in the history curriculum had commanded my attention as this did. I was thoroughly hooked.

Fifteen months later I started my first theology degree.

My interest in Christian theology and ethics, therefore, has never been simply academic. From the very beginning, my theological study has been driven by a desire — which has gradually revealed itself as a vocation — to put myself in the position of being able to speak in the world at once with Christian integrity and with practical wisdom.

Accordingly, as a doctoral student I was drawn to the thought of Karl Barth by the prospect of learning from a Christian vision of moral and political life that is theologically comprehensive (as well as basically orthodox). I was not disappointed. Nevertheless, I did find myself dissatisfied at the indeterminate way in which Barth's theologically generated ethical concepts often hover frustratingly above the concrete earth of complex moral and political problems, or at the sometimes haphazard manner of his leaping from theological premise to moral rule or concrete judgment. Hence my simultaneous attraction to Scholastic methodicality and casuistry.

My dissatisfaction with much post-Barthian Christian ethical thinking runs along parallel lines. It seems to me that recent Christian ethics has tended to be strong in its determination to achieve theologically critical distance from what passes for common moral sense by immersing itself in the traditions of Christian moral thought. It has often performed poorly, however, at bringing the resources of its historical mining to engage at close, honest, and considerate quarters with present issues of public policy. It is true, of course, that engaging with public policy is not the only way of causing Christian faith to shape the world for good. Arguably, it is more important to foster an alternative ethos within the churches, which can show forth what salutary social and political life looks like. Nevertheless, the rest of the world is being daily misshapen by decisions about public policy, and Christian ethics should care to reserve some of its energy for engaging critically and constructively with those, too.

Of course, some manifestations of Christian ethics have done that. I think, for example, of *Faith in the City,* the 1985 report of the Archbishop of Canterbury's Commission on Urban Priority Areas, or *Changing Britain,* the 1987 publication of the Church of England's Board for Social Responsibility.[1] Each of these deals with pressing social problems in Britain: *Faith in the City* with urban deprivation, *Changing Britain* with cultural and moral pluralism. Neither of them did so, however, with moral concepts that had drunk at all deeply from the wells of the Christian moral theological tradition. The result was that their moral analysis and criticism was too spellbound by current liberal-left common sense. As I wrote in the wake of the publication of *Faith in the City*:

> If we may take *Faith in the City* as symptomatic (and it is certainly not wholly eccentric), then we can say of social ethics in the Church of England today what has recently been asserted of her current conception of her political role: that she has yet to take seriously the intellectual task of developing a fundamentally *theological* understanding of it.[2]

It seems to me, therefore, that recent Christian ethics has tended to present us with a choice between two options: either a "conservative" biblical and theological seriousness, which is shy of attending too closely to public policy; or "liberal" engagement with public policy, which is theologically thin and bland. This is a choice that I have long resisted making, and it is the purpose of this book to justify that resistance and to articulate a third way.

---

1. *Faith in the City: A Call for Action by Church and Nation,* A Report of the Archbishop of Canterbury's Commission on Urban Priority Areas (London: Church House Publishing, 1985); *Changing Britain,* A Report of the Board of Social Responsibility of the General Synod of the Church of England (London: Church House Publishing, 1987).

2. Nigel Biggar, *Theological Politics: A Critique of "Faith in the City,"* the Report of the Archbishop of Canterbury's Commission on Urban Priority Areas (1985), Latimer Studies 29-30 (Oxford: Latimer House, 1988), p. 64.

CHAPTER 1

Integrity, Not Distinctiveness

Concern for integrity has been one of the abiding preoccupations of Christian ethics since World War II. It has also been one of its chief signs of vigor. In the 1950s many Roman Catholic moral theologians reacted against their Neo-Scholastic heritage, with its legalistic focus on obligation and its philosophical emphasis on the law of nature. Instead, they sought out a more genuinely evangelical, salvific vision of moral life — a vision that eventually found official expression in the Second Vatican Council's 1965 injunction that moral theology should take its cue from Scripture.[1] Shortly after that, in Protestant circles Paul Ramsey inveighed against Joseph Fletcher's reduction of Christian ethics to a utilitarian concept of love, invoking instead the biblical concept of deontic covenant-faithfulness.[2] Then, in the middle of the following decade, Stanley Hauerwas began his lifelong reaction against the preoccupation of ethics with the abstract analysis of quandaries, to the neglect of the right formation of the self in the light of a larger and specifically theological worldview.[3] Hauerwas's reaction acquired the dimensions of a trend

1. See Vincent MacNamara, *Faith and Ethics: Recent Roman Catholicism* (Dublin: Gill and MacMillan, 1985), chap. 1.

2. Paul Ramsey, "The Case of the Curious Exception," in *Norm and Context in Christian Ethics,* ed. Gene Outka and Paul Ramsey (New York: Scribner's, 1968), pp. 81, 119, 125.

3. E.g., Stanley Hauerwas, *Character and the Christian Life: A Study in Theological Ethics* (San Antonio: Trinity University Press, 1975), esp. pp. 7-8; see also Hauerwas, *The Peaceable Kingdom: A Primer in Christian Ethics* (Notre Dame, IN: Notre Dame University Press, 1983), chap. 2.

when it was reinforced in the 1980s and 1990s by a revival of Anglo-Saxon (and especially British) interest in the moral theology of Karl Barth, whose insistence on the integration of ethics into Christian dogmatics is unrivaled in its stringency.[4]

Much of the rising concern to secure the Christian character of Christian ethics has been provoked and sustained by the postwar challenges posed to traditional norms in the West by liberal thinking on sexual and political matters, and by utilitarian thinking on medical ones. Because such thinking rapidly achieved the status of common sense, Christians have been pressed to develop an ethical language with which to express their doubts and their alternatives; and this has led them to revisit the theological roots and premodern sources of Christian ethics in search of critical distance and leverage. Oliver O'Donovan's magisterial construal of the history of biblical and medieval political thought is a prime example of this.[5]

To talk about a concern for the integrity of Christian ethics, however, is to speak too vaguely. The concern is for *theological* integrity, for it is the theological dimension of Christian ethics that sets it most obviously apart from liberal and utilitarian common sense. Liberal and utilitarian ethics in their culturally dominant forms are studiously nonreligious, often assertively antireligious. Accordingly, a Christian ethic that would respond to them with something more than an echo must understand its own theological sources and how those sources bear on moral life.

And yet, even to speak of theological integrity does not quite capture the nature of the recent abiding concern of Christian ethics. There are different readings of how theology should bear on ethics. For example, some moral theologians appeal largely to the doctrine of creation to ground an affirmation of given moral reality or order — that is, an

4. E.g, the essays by Nigel Biggar, John Webster, Stanley Hauerwas, and Rowan Williams in *Reckoning with Barth: Essays in Commemoration of the Centenary of Karl Barth's Birth,* ed. Nigel Biggar (Oxford: Mowbray, 1988); Nigel Biggar, *The Hastening That Waits: Karl Barth's Ethics* (Oxford: Clarendon Press, 1993; 1995); and John Webster, *Barth's Ethics of Reconciliation* (Cambridge: Cambridge University Press, 1995).

5. See Oliver O'Donovan, *The Desire of the Nations: Rediscovering the Roots of Political Theology* (Cambridge: Cambridge University Press, 1996); see also O'Donovan, *The Ways of Judgment,* the 2003 Bampton Lectures (Grand Rapids: Eerdmans, 2005).

ethic of "natural law." Others make much play of the creaturely nature and fallen condition of human beings in order to ground a "realistic" ethic in which the virtue of prudence looms large. Still others invoke Jesus to ground a norm of self-sacrificial love. All of these can claim to integrate ethics into theology, but none of them meets the relevant concern. This is best described as a concern, not just for theological integrity, but for theological *narrative* integrity. The theological doctrines of Creation and the Fall are the easiest to correlate with secularist thinking: even unbelievers sometimes recognize the claims of a given moral reality, concede the limits of human control, or acknowledge the disturbing propensity of human beings toward wicked behavior. Likewise, an ethical reading of the significance of Jesus in terms of his teaching and exemplifying a certain kind of love is necessary: one does not need to be a believer to admit the claims of love, even in the form of self-sacrifice, and to see it manifested extraordinarily in Jesus of Nazareth. These are the easy parts. More difficult to reconcile with secularist thinking are those elements of the story that the Christian Bible and Christian orthodoxy tell about the world, which assert the saving power of God *in* it. These include a reading of Jesus not just as a moral teacher and exemplar but also as God incarnate, as well as the eschatological hope that God will save and fulfill the world at the end of history. Therefore, the concern for theological integrity that has animated so much Christian ethics in recent decades is a concern that ethics be governed by the *whole* story, including those christological and eschatological parts of it that attest the salvific presence of God in history and in its conclusion. The concern for integrity is certainly a concern that ethics be integrated into theology, but it is more than just that. It is also a concern that the theology into which ethics is integrated comprises a salvation narrative that is complete, and that it is therefore one in which faith in the saving activity of God in history is not sheepishly downplayed.

This element of the concern for the integrity of Christian ethics, then, represents an orthodox reaction against a liberal apologetic strategy that has long sought to appease religion's cultured despisers by sacrificing — or at least equivocating over — traditional Christian soteriology. Hauerwas's criticism of Reinhold Niebuhr provides us with a case in point. His complaint is that Niebuhr, overimpressed by the claims of "modern science" to have banished supernatural activity from a clockwork universe governed by mechanical laws, lost his theological nerve and dissolved theology into anthropology.[6] Those expressions that have the form of statements about God's action in history are in fact "myths" expressive of eternal truths about human being and existence. Miracles understood as the violation of the laws of natural causation are no longer credible, Niebuhr tells us, and so we cannot "believe in the virgin birth, and we have difficulty with the physical resurrection of Christ."[7] Instead, he says, we should regard the Resurrection as a symbol by which "the Christian faith hopes for an eternity which transfigures, but does not annul, the temporal process."[8] Over against this Bultmannian reinterpretation, Hauerwas asserts an orthodox soteriology, which, in cleaving to a physical resurrection, not only expresses hope for transfiguration but puts the ground back under its feet. It also generates an ethic inspired by such hope to raise its eyes beyond Niebuhrian, sin-chastened prudence.

The dual concern that ethics be integrated with theology, and that this theology maintain its orthodox integrity, I thoroughly applaud. While the existentialist anthropologies of Rudolf Bultmann and Paul Tillich and Reinhold Niebuhr have long gripped me, I have always been puzzled by their soteriological equivocation. It redounds to Niebuhr's credit that he persisted in clinging to hope for the transfiguration of the temporal world; but quite how he could do this, having mythologized the bodily resurrection of Jesus, I just do not see. A metaphorical resurrection is really not of much help to beings whose death is no metaphor. Still, today we have advantages that theologians working in the first seven decades of the twentieth century lacked. Nowadays, with the dissemination of post-Newtonian science and the resurgence of metaphys-

6. Stanley Hauerwas, *With the Grain of the Universe: The Church's Witness and Natural Theology* (Grand Rapids: Brazos, 2001), pp. 109-10, 120, 140.

7. Reinhold Niebuhr, "Coherence, Incoherence, and Christian Faith," in *Christian Realism and Political Problems* (London: Faber and Faber, 1953), p. 186, cited in Hauerwas, *With the Grain*, p. 129.

8. Reinhold Niebuhr, "The Church and the End of History," in *Faith and History: A Comparison of Christian and Modern Views of History* (New York: Scribner's, 1949), p. 237, cited in Hauerwas, *With the Grain*, p. 129n.35.

ics and theism, talk about God and his extraordinary activity in the world of time and space is much easier to justify.

The concern for theological integrity plumbs yet further depths. Beyond the integration of Christian ethics into theology, and beyond the identification of that theology as structured by the *whole* biblical narrative, and thus including an orthodox, historical soteriology and eschatology — beyond that, Hauerwas contends for something yet more specific. One of his constant complaints against "natural law" ethics, be they Roman Catholic or Niebuhrian,[9] is that their methodology has the result "that theological convictions about Jesus are not directly relevant to concrete ethical analysis."[10] When Hauerwas says "Jesus," however, he does not mean just any Christology. Ethics whose practical norms are directly shaped by the doctrine of the Incarnation, for example, as in Anglican Christian socialism, would not satisfy him. "Incarnation," he writes, "is not an adequate summary of the story" (p. 57). It is too abstract, too little historical and particular. The same applies even to the principle of neighbor-love (p. 60). Instead, Hauerwas argues that to encapsulate the story of Jesus in a manner sufficiently historical, we have to specify neighbor-love in the light of the cross and speak, with ascending precision, in terms of service, peacemaking, humility, vulnerability, renunciation, dispossession, forgiving enemies, and nonviolence (pp. 76, 80, 81, 85, 87ff.).

Now, of course, a Christian ethic must allow the moral significance of Jesus to shape it directly — but only at the appropriate points. It seems to me, for example, that whereas Jesus' teaching and example has something explicit to say about how we should react when we suffer injustice — namely, with forgiveness — it does not bear so directly on how we should react when we suffer cancer.[11] I also agree on the need to capture the moral significance of Jesus in terms that do justice to the historical particularity of his story and that are exegetically responsible.

---

9. Hauerwas writes of Niebuhr that his "understanding of the law of love is an attempt to develop a natural law ethic" (*With the Grain*, p. 134).

10. Hauerwas, *Peaceable Kingdom*, p. 55. In this paragraph, page references to this work appear in parentheses in the text.

11. See Nigel Biggar, *Aiming to Kill: The Ethics of Suicide and Euthanasia* (London: Darton, Longman, and Todd, 2004), pp. 49-55.

I have argued elsewhere that we should be less slapdash than Barth is in his lectures on the command of God the reconciler, where he tells us that Jesus was in favor of "human rights, human freedom, and human peace" and that he was against political absolutism, materialism, rigid ideologies, and disordered powers such as pleasure — not to mention technology, fashion, sport, and transportation.[12] I agree, too, that part of the normative import of Jesus' story is the refusal of violence. Where I disagree with Hauerwas is in reading this refusal as implying an absolute rule, always and everywhere applicable. Yes, Jesus refused the violence that issues from nationalist idolatry; and yes, he enjoined the forgiveness of enemies.[13] Not all violence is inspired by idolatrous nationalism, however, and forgiveness-as-compassion is compatible with the use of violent force (as I have argued elsewhere).[14]

One final aspect of the concern for the integrity of Christian ethics remains to be mentioned, namely, that ethical reflection find practical expression, particularly in the corporate life of the Christian church. Christianity is not just another system of belief, Hauerwas tells us,[15] and Christian ethics is not just an intellectual discipline, but "a form of reflection in service to a community."[16] Surely this has to be true of any moral theological reflection that takes its own content at all seriously.

The concern that ethics be integrated with theology, that this theology maintain its biblical and orthodox integrity, that it therefore include a historical soteriology and eschatology as well as an anthropology, that the definitive story of Jesus be allowed a direct bearing on appropriate conduct, that this story be read so as to do justice to its historical particularity, and that ethical reflection be ordered toward shaping the life of the church — all of this is perfectly proper. If Christians believe, as they should, that there is a God, that he is a distinct reality and not just an anthropological symbol, that he wears the face of Jesus

12. Nigel Biggar, "Karl Barth's Ethics Revisited," in *Commanding Grace: Karl Barth's Theological Ethics*, ed. Daniel Migliore (Grand Rapids: Eerdmans, 2010), pp. 42-45.

13. Hauerwas, *Peaceable Kingdom*, pp. 79, 83-84.

14. For further explanation, see my "Forgiving Enemies in Ireland," *Journal of Religious Ethics* 36, no. 4 (December 2008): 560-64.

15. Stanley Hauerwas, "On Keeping Theological Ethics Theological," in *The Hauerwas Reader* (Durham: Duke University Press, 2001), p. 72.

16. Hauerwas, *Peaceable Kingdom*, p. 54.

of Nazareth, that he suffered judicial murder while looking with compassion upon his murderers, that his is the power that raised the crucified Jesus bodily from the dead, and that hence there is eschatological hope for a perishing world — if Christians believe all this, then they should take care to work out their ethics in terms of their creed. They, along with everyone else, must construe the truth according to their best lights; and they must bear witness to it. Of course, they might be mistaken in what they see and assert. But if they are not mistaken, and if they fail to tell what they see, then they have failed in love for their neighbors and robbed them of the opportunity to apprehend a real benefit. Christians should tell it as they see it.

The question of how best to tell it, however — the question of how to communicate effectively what one believes to be true — is another, distinct question. The art of successful persuasion might advise Christians against telling the whole truth at once or at first. It might advise against referring to theological premises before they have made efforts to explain what they mean and why those premises matter. It might advise an oblique approach, avoiding the use of theological clichés that incline listeners to yawn rather than startle them into reflection. Such rhetorical tactics need not be a symptom of lack of nerve. On the contrary, they can be an expression of sensitivity to the otherness of others and of a readiness to place oneself in their shoes, in order to discern how best to walk them into one's own vision of things. Sequence matters: an assertion that makes no sense at the beginning of an argumentative journey can make good sense at the end. Rhetorical canniness need not be a sign of evasion. It can be an expression of love — both for the neighbor and for the truth that one would have the neighbor see.

This is all very important (and I will talk further about it in Chapter 4); but it is not the first thing. The first thing for Christian ethicists is to articulate ethics in a manner that coheres with the theological convictions that are basic to Christian identity. If they do not do this, then the point of being a *Christian* ethicist is, of course, lost. No good purpose is served when Christian ethics plays sycophant to whatever passes for common sense. No one benefits when it consistently amounts to an echo. Karl Barth was absolutely correct: Christian ethics "must always

7

be absolutely resolved to stick to its colours"; "[it] must not . . . disarm its distinctive Whence? and Whither? in order to assure itself a place in the sun of general ethical discussion."[17]

So the recent concern for the theological integrity of Christian ethics is perfectly proper. Integrity, however, is not the same as distinctiveness. One is a virtue; the other is an accident of history. If the Christian ethicist maintains his theological integrity, then there are bound to be occasions when he will say things that differ from what other people are saying. Since not everyone shares his theological premises, and since these premises shape moral vision and life, then his ethics will sometimes be distinctive. Sometimes, but not always. Those who do not share his theological beliefs might nevertheless reach similar ethical conclusions by a different route. Sometimes that route will be equally adequate, and sometimes it will not; but the result is more or less the same. Whether or not what the Christian ethicist has to say is distinctive depends on the happenstance of whom he is talking with and what he is talking about; it is a matter of historical accident. Distinctiveness is no measure of integrity.

It might be that the Christian ethicist is operating in a social and political environment that he considers generally inimical to the living of the good life. If, for example, he is a pacifist and believes national loyalty per se to be idolatrous, then his vision of moral life is going to be constantly distinctive in a society such as the United States, where patriotic feeling and expression is normal, and where government is not averse to using lethal force in support of its political aims. In that context pacifist distinctiveness would be a mark of theological integrity — but only in that context. For if our pacifist were to be relocated in contemporary postnationalist Germany, for example, it would become far more difficult to tell his Christian ethic from common sense.[18]

---

17. Karl Barth, *Church Dogmatics,* ed. G. W. Bromiley and T. F. Torrance, vol. 2, *The Doctrine of God,* pt. 2, trans. J. C. Campbell et al. (Edinburgh: T. & T. Clark, 1957), p. 524.

18. I do not say that Christian pacifism would appear identical to, say, humanist pacifism. The Christian pacifist might justify his refusal of violence as an act of faithful discipleship, which takes its cue from Jesus' (alleged) example and is sustained by the eschatological hope that God will make things turn out right in the end. The humanist pacifist would probably appeal instead to the evils, futility, and counterproductivity of violence and argue that greater patience, sympathy, and understanding are alternative, preferable,

For this reason I cannot quite endorse Hauerwas's general call for Christians to let their peculiar narrative produce a church that is distinct from "the world."[19] I do not disagree that Christian ethics needs to display the moral difference that Christian theological commitments make.[20] However, if liberal theologians such as Niebuhr have failed to articulate *all* that difference, they have nevertheless succeeded in articulating some of it.[21] And if the likes of Paul Ramsey have sometimes downplayed the theological elements of their ethics for the sake of being persuasive in public discussion, that might have been an expression of rhetorical love rather than a lack of theological nerve.[22] It might also have been because on those occasions theology had no direct bearing on the matter at hand. Of course, the Church is distinct from the World, since by definition "the World" (capital *W*) denotes that which is hostile to "the Church" (capital *C*); and there have been times in history when these ideal types have become actualities. But there have also been times when the lines have been less clearly drawn, not because actual churches have failed to be and to say what they should, but because their cultural environment has either borne their imprint or seen universal moral reality straight. The actual world is not always hostile. Sometimes it includes believers or half-believers or benign skeptics. Sometimes it perceives the given moral order and its practical implications accurately. And because we live in the *saeculum,* the secular age when the tares are allowed to mingle with the wheat, members of the Church may be found in the actual world, and members of the World may be found in actual churches. The world is not always the World; in which case, actual churches should not always be distinct from it.

Integrity, not distinctiveness, is the point. How, then, do we achieve it? How do we achieve narrative theological integrity and maintain it?

---

and genuine solvents of conflict. Nevertheless, if the Christian were to ask himself *why* God-in-Jesus turns his face against violence — or what it is about violence that causes God to eschew it — then his answer is likely to operate in terms similar to the humanist's.

19. Hauerwas, *Peaceable Kingdom,* p. 60.
20. Hauerwas, "On Keeping Theological Ethics Theological," p. 73.
21. Hauerwas, *With the Grain,* p. 231.
22. Hauerwas, "On Keeping Theological Ethics Theological," pp. 65, 67-68.

Obviously, by thinking hard about the bearing of theological topics on moral matters, by discerning what the moral implications of theological concepts and doctrines are, and by tracing how these shape moral questions and answers. Sometimes the bearing will be direct. So, for example, the Christian concept of the world as the creation of one rational and benevolent God directly implies the existence of a given moral order that precedes all human choices and to which human creatures are responsible in their choosing. Likewise, the belief that the teaching and conduct of Jesus represents the will of God and the way to salvation directly prescribes that any response to injustice be shaped by forgiveness (in some form).[23]

Nevertheless, theology does not touch directly on every important point of a moral argument. For example, in considering the question of the morality of physicians killing their patients upon request (that is, voluntary euthanasia), a pivotal and controversial issue is whether a substantial (and not merely verbal) moral distinction can be made between the following two cases. In both of them the patient is terminally ill and in severe distress. In one case, the physician seeks to relieve the patient by administering an appropriate dosage of a painkilling drug, while knowing that there is a very high probability that the dosage will also kill the patient. In the other case, the physician, judging that nothing less than a lethal dosage of drug will relieve the patient's distress, resolves to kill the patient. Utilitarian philosophers deny that there is a meaningful difference between, on the one hand, an intention to relieve pain by means that one knows will probably kill, and, on the other hand, an intention to kill in order to relieve pain. Insofar as the moral theologian sees the human individual's life as an occasion for making herself fit for the world to come, he is theologically predisposed to regard the agent's intention as an important determinant of the moral quality of her act. For in intending something evil, we want it; and in wanting it, we bind ourselves to it; and in binding ourselves to it, we corrupt ourselves by it. So the theologian is more likely than a secularist

23. That is, at least in the form of forgiveness-as-compassion, if not in the form of forgiveness-as-absolution. For an explanation of this distinction, see my "Forgiving Enemies in Ireland," pp. 560-64.

philosopher to care about the quality of the agent's intention. However, the fact that theology makes intention in general a serious moral consideration does not mean that it has anything to contribute, when it comes to the important task of deciding what makes it valid to distinguish an evil that is intentionally caused from one that is caused deliberately but unintentionally. Is an intended evil one that I cause directly or immediately? Or is it one that I can foresee as highly probable or certain? Or is it one that falls within my "plan"? In the face of this kind of question, the moral theologian finds himself simply doing moral philosophy, and quite appropriately so.[24]

Too often, however, contemporary Christian ethicists who are concerned about theological integrity insist on keeping ethics on too short a leash. They become suspicious whenever theology's control is not direct and immediate. This is partly the expression of an admirable concern to ensure that ethics is sufficiently shaped by theological premises. It might also be the expression, however, of a less admirable overestimation of theology's self-sufficiency and underestimation of what nontheological reflection has to offer. Whatever the cause, the result is argumentation that moves impatiently from theological affirmation to premature moral conclusion.[25] An infamous instance is supplied by Karl Barth, whose influence is contemporary, even if he himself is not. This instance comprises the set of "analogies" that Barth makes, in his 1946 essay "The Christian Community and the Civil Community," between Christian dogmatic tenets and ethical positions. To take one example, Barth tells us that since "the Church lives from the disclosure of the true God and His revelation," it follows as "an inevitable political corollary . . . that the Church is the sworn enemy of all . . . secret diplomacy."[26] We see here the dogmatic premise; we see, too, the ethical conclusion; and we hear the *assertion* of logical necessity binding

---

24. As did I in *Aiming to Kill,* chap. 3, "The Morality of Acts," esp. pp. 71-88.

25. What now follows is a considerably revised and expanded version of part of my essay "Saving the 'Secular': The Public Vocation of Moral Theology," *Journal of Religious Ethics* 37, no. 1 (March 2009): 170-72.

26. Karl Barth, "The Christian Community and the Civil Community," in *Community, State, and Church: Three Essays,* ed. Will Herberg (Gloucester, MA: Peter Smith, 1968), p. 176.

them together. What we miss is the moral analysis of different kinds of openness, articulating what is good about God's revelation of himself to human creatures, explaining why this is analogous to the open publicity of diplomatic negotiations, and thereby demonstrating what is wrong with secret diplomacy. As it stands, the corollary is not only a long way short of logical inevitability; it is risible in its crudity.

Less crude, more contemporary, but nonetheless problematic are those arguments — be they from conservative Roman Catholics such as Germain Grisez or from Lutherans such as Martin Honecker — that since the theological doctrines of Creation, the Incarnation, and the Resurrection all affirm that bodiliness is valuable and essential to human being, therefore Christians may not distinguish between its biological and personal dimensions, deeming some biologically living human beings (such as Tony Bland[27]) to be nonpersons and undeserving of life-saving treatment.[28] As it stands, this is a non sequitur: for to say

27. Tony Bland was among those injured on April 15, 1989, in the disaster at the Hillsborough football stadium in Sheffield, where almost one hundred spectators were crushed to death. Bland survived, but his lungs were crushed and punctured, and the supply of oxygen to his brain was interrupted, causing irreversible damage to its higher, cortical centers. The condition in which he lingered for just under four years in hospital is known as "persistent vegetative state" (PVS). Its distinctive features are that the brain stem remains alive and functioning, but not the brain's cortex. The former supports basic bodily functions; the latter supports consciousness. Accordingly, the PVS patient is able to breathe and digest unaided, and he is capable of reflex movement, especially in response to painful stimuli. However, lacking cognitive function, he can neither see, nor hear, nor feel pain and emotion, nor communicate. Nor can he feed himself. In Bland's case, the medical consensus was that, like most patients in PVS, he would never recover. After all, his cortex had liquefied. Both his parents and his doctor wanted to stop his artificial feeding (by tube through the nose) and the treatment of his infections by antibiotics; but they were advised that, if artificial feeding was stopped, the doctor might be prosecuted for homicide. In order to obtain an authoritative legal ruling, the trust that ran the hospital then applied to the High Court for a declaration that the cessation of feeding and antibiotics would be lawful. The Official Solicitor opposed the application, eventually appealing to the highest court in England, the House of Lords. In 1993, the Law Lords finally dismissed the appeal. Bland's tube-feeding was stopped, and he died a few days later on March 3.

28. Germain Grisez, *The Way of the Lord Jesus*, vol. 2, *Living a Christian Life* (Quincy, IL: Franciscan Press, 1993), chap. 8, question A: "Why Should Human Life Always be Treated with Reverence?" (pp. 460-69); Martin Honecker, "Sterbehilfe und Euthanasie aus theologischer Sicht," in *Lebensverkürzung, Tötung und Serientötung — eine inter-*

that there cannot be a person where there is no body is one thing; but to say that where there is a living human body there is necessarily a person is quite another. That bodies are necessary for persons does not make them sufficient.[29] The theological premises here do not add up to the moral conclusion.

A similar problem can be found in Richard Hays's book *The Moral Vision of the New Testament,* which attracted high praise upon its publication in 1996 and is now widely admired as a classic. Hays shares the view of the Hauerwasian school that moral theology must stick close to the "biblical narrative" if it is to remain genuinely Christian. He correctly observes that when ethical concepts are abstracted from that narrative, they are vulnerable to being understood in ways that are alien to fundamental Christian presuppositions.[30] For example, the concept of love means one thing in the light of the Gospel stories of Jesus' crucifixion, but something rather different in the light of soap-opera romances. From this, however, Hays wrongly concludes that moral theology should think its way to moral judgments by drawing "imaginative analogies" directly between the biblical stories and our own situations, rather than by abstracting general principles and then applying them methodically to cases (pp. 298-304). It is true that he acknowledges that abstract principles are one of the New Testament's modes of ethical discourse, that all the New Testament's modes of ethical discourse should be incorporated into the church's ethical teaching (p. 294), that principles should — and presumably can — find a place within the story of God's redemption of the world through Jesus Christ, and that the paradigmatic or analogical mode is primary or preeminent rather than exclusive (pp. 295, 339). Nevertheless, he also tells us — inconsistently — that it is impossible to separate out timeless truth from culturally conditioned elements (p. 299), that "a Christian ethic that seeks to be faithfully responsive to the New Testament texts *will not move abstractly away* from the form in which the texts present themselves to us" (p. 294; italics added), and that we need

---

disciplinäre Analyse der "Euthanasie," ed. Manfred Oehmichen (Lübeck: Schmidt-Römhild, 1996), p. 79.

29. Biggar, *Aiming to Kill,* pp. 32-35, 176n.45.

30. Richard Hays, *The Moral Vision of the New Testament* (Edinburgh: T. & T. Clark, 1996), p. 202. Hereafter, page references to this work appear in parentheses in the text.

to honor the particularity of the texts by moving between their world and ours by way of metaphors and *"without* subjecting them to analytic procedures that abstract general principles from them" (p. 300; italics added). Moreover, it is noteworthy that while Hays is willing to acknowledge those rules and principles that the New Testament authors themselves have already formulated — for example, turning the other cheek, loving one's enemies — he nowhere owns fresh ones that his own reflection on the New Testament has generated.

Part of Hays's emphasis on metaphor-making is driven by a legitimate concern that Christian ethics retain the critical, life-changing impact of the New Testament. Metaphors, he tells us, are incongruous conjunctions of two images that shock us into novel thought: "Metaphors reshape perception"; to "'understand' . . . parables is to be changed by them" (pp. 300-301). Without any doubt, this prophetic mode is an important — even a basic one — for Christian ethics. Sometimes the Christian ethicist needs to challenge idols, unsettle assumptions, and disturb complacencies. To take an example supplied by Hays himself, sometimes she will need to protest against the idol of national security (p. 303). But prophecy and protest should not be the only modes of which the Christian ethicist is capable. Sometimes she will also need to think carefully and analytically about the proper responsibilities of government and about what is permissible in defense of national security and under what conditions. Sometimes she will need to shuffle off the shoes of the prophet and step into those of the policymaker.

Another reason why Hays prefers moral reasoning by metaphor or analogy is that he is keen to preclude evasion by abstraction. He resists the Enlightenment and Kantian tendency to "translate" biblical claims about God's particular salvific action in history into suprahistorical truths about the universal law of practical reason (p. 300). And rightly so — in my theologically orthodox view. However, there is a different kind of abstraction that he also — and in my view, wrongly — resists: namely, that which draws general principles of Christian ethics out of particular injunctions in the New Testament. His concern here is that such a process is a means of evading the text's stringent moral demand. Accordingly, he forbids us to follow Clement of Alexandria in turning the injunction to sell possessions and give alms (Luke 12:33) into a principle of inner detachment. Likewise, he protests against Reinhold Niebuhr's turning the Sermon on the Mount's teaching against violence into an ideal of love that can sometimes sanction it (p. 294).

It is surely correct to say that a principle of inner detachment that is not expected to express itself in acts of costly generosity would be suspect of misrepresenting the meaning of the Gospel text. However, if we are not to take the injunction as a rule applying always and everywhere — and Hays does not say that we should — then we are faced with the question of what its implication for Christian behavior actually is. And how else can we give an answer except in terms of a general rule of conduct? If the virtue of inner detachment alone does not suffice, then perhaps an inner detachment sustained and strengthened by periodic expressions of rash generosity would.

As for the Sermon on the Mount, Hays objects to Niebuhr's generalization only because it contradicts his own. Hays takes the Sermon not merely to enjoin nonviolence on particular occasions, but to assert a rule against violence that applies always and everywhere. That is why he resists Niebuhr's inference of a principle of love that is consonant with acts of violence in defense of justice. But what this implies is that the issue is not *whether* to generalize, but *how.*

Besides, metaphor-making and analogy-constructing are not alternatives to analysis and abstraction. An analogue is at once similar to and different from the paradigm; and an apposite analogy is similar in all the significant respects. In order to make my analogy apposite, therefore, I must first analyze the paradigm and pick out — abstract — its universally significant elements. (This analysis and abstraction need not be articulated; it might be, and in most cases it will be, intuitive.) For example, in order to discern how my behavior here and now should correspond to Jesus' conduct during his passion, I must first decide how to characterize Jesus' conduct. I have to try to encapsulate it. Should I read it as a repudiation of religious nationalism? Or as a noble act of suicide? Or as an act of love? Or more specifically as an act of self-sacrifice? Or more specifically yet, as an act of forbearance and forgiveness? Whatever my interpretation, I cannot avoid abstracting from the story a kind of conduct that is morally normative. That is, I cannot avoid analyzing the story into an abstract moral principle. Nor, in fact, does Richard

Hays. For while he declines to read the cross in the vague terms of a principle of love, he nevertheless chooses to read it instead in the more definite terms of a rule of nonviolence. Moreover, because he officially eschews the analysis of abstract concepts in favor of the direct intuition of "imaginative analogies," he shields his own abstract principle from critical analysis. Is "nonviolence" really the best summary of what Jesus taught and did? Should we not follow Saint Paul in making moral distinctions between violence in the service of private interests and lethal force used for the public good (Rom. 13:1-4), and between sinful and sinless anger (Eph. 4:26)? And should we not then specify Jesus as repudiating, not all uses of lethal force under any conceivable circumstance, but specifically the private use of violence in the service of hateful, vengeful, and imprudent nationalist revolt? Did Jesus really mean to prohibit, say, Tony Blair from sending armed troops to Sierra Leone in 1999 in order to prevent diamond-greedy, drug-crazed, limb-chopping rebels from seizing control of the country? Is this case really analogous to Jesus' passion? Is the kind of violence that Jesus repudiated the same, morally speaking, as what the British soldiers adopted?

Richard Hays's recommendation that the Christian ethicist make moral judgments by way of direct analogies between the biblical text and his situation here and now, *instead of* conceptual analysis and abstraction, encourages a false choice. Furthermore, it threatens to confine Christian ethics to the prophetic mode, to railing at obvious idols, while robbing it of the tools for crafting the subtle moral assessment of difficult policy choices.

Hays's suspicion of abstraction and conceptual analysis is consonant with a long-standing Protestant suspicion of casuistry — that is, the methodical "application" of ethical principles and rules to concrete cases.[31] At least since World War II, Protestant theologians have complained that casuistry abstracts the process of making moral decisions from the theological history — from the theological narrative context — of the moral agent. Hence Karl Barth's insistence in the 1940s that all ethical reflection should be understood as preliminary to the event of

---

31. See Nigel Biggar, "A Case for Casuistry in the Church," *Modern Theology* 6, no. 1 (October 1989).

encounter between the sinful human creature and the Creator, who commands with a view to saving.[32] Hence, too, Paul Lehmann's argument in the 1960s that Christians should avoid the casuist's preoccupation with calculating rational solutions to moral quandaries, with its consequent obscuring of the larger theological historical context of the moral agent as a sinner whom God has already acted to save, and seek, instead, to make his action correspond to the history of what God is doing in complex, dynamic situations to humanize the world by building up *koinonia*.[33] Likewise, Hauerwas's lament in the 1980s about the tendency of Roman Catholic moral theologians to so immerse themselves in the analysis of acts and the adjudication of cases that they are "seldom required to make direct theological appeals,"[34] and his objection to their casuistry for failing to notice how the Christian narrative informs the very description of cases.[35]

This Protestant criticism is well taken. It is perfectly true that some moral analyses of cases use norms and descriptions that are inadequately shaped by what has been revealed in the biblical narrative (and quintessentially in the story of Jesus) about the human good, its defense, and its promotion. Such inadequacy, however, is not a necessary feature of abstraction or analysis or casuistry. It is perfectly possible for these to be scrupulously mindful of relevant biblical and theological considerations. Why, then, does Richard Hays not recognize this? One reason may be that he tends to associate casuistry and all its analytical distinctions, via the natural-law tradition, with the doctrine of just war. This doctrine distinguishes different moral kinds of use of lethal force: what is vindictive, premature, disproportionate, and indiscriminate from what is peace-seeking, forbearing, proportionate, and discriminating. The former it judges contrary to the moral significance of Jesus, but not the latter. Hays, however, is convinced that the New Testament

---

32. Barth, *Church Dogmatics,* II/2, pp. 676-78.

33. Paul Lehmann, *Ethics in a Christian Context* (New York: Harper and Row, 1963), pp. 319-22, 143.

34. Hauerwas, *Peaceable Kingdom,* p. 51.

35. Hauerwas, *Peaceable Kingdom,* pp. 117, 124, 125-26. To his credit, Hauerwas does not deny the need to adjudicate difficult cases (pp. 120, 123): "The question is not whether to have or not to have casuistry, but what kind we should have" (pp. 130-31).

enjoins pacifism — that is, the absolute and unconditional repudiation of the use of lethal force. Accordingly, he regards such distinctions as unbiblical and un-Christian, and thus he mistrusts the reasoning that has produced them.[36] If his judgment were correct, however, the problem would still not lie in the abstraction of principles from the biblical narrative, nor in the elaboration of moral distinctions, nor in the analysis of cases. Rather, it would lie in the interpretation of the New Testament and in the resultant content of the principles that are abstracted, elaborated, and applied.[37] Even if we were to grant Hays's point of view, the proper moral of the story would be the need for abstraction and analysis to be appropriately governed by biblical and theological premises — and not their eschewal for the intuitive drawing of direct, unadulterated analogies.

On this point, it seems to me, Barth got it quite right — albeit more in principle than in practice. As I have noted above, on the one hand, some of Barth's ethics do suffer in practice from an excessive zeal for thinking theologically, for referring everything directly to God, and for tending to ignore what does not lend itself to such reference. I presume to call this "excessive" because the world that God has created is distinct and relatively free. The Creator and his creation are always related; and the latter always depends on the former and is responsible to him. But the Creator and his creation are not the same thing; they are not identical.[38] I say this on several grounds: first, my immediate experience of the world, where I do not find myself constantly and directly confronted with God; second, my experience of love, which always

36. See his dismissal of "logic-chopping" in Richard Hays, "Narrate and Embody: A Response to Nigel Biggar," *Studies in Christian Ethics* 22, no. 2 (May 2009): 195, and, more generally, pp. 192-95.

37. As it happens, I have argued against Richard Hays that the New Testament is better comprehended in terms of just-war doctrine than in terms of pacifism, and that it bears the moral distinctions that the doctrine makes. See Nigel Biggar, "Specify and Distinguish! Interpreting the New Testament on 'Non-violence,'" *Studies in Christian Ethics* 22, no. 2 (May 2009); and "The New Testament and Violence: Round Two," in *Studies in Christian Ethics* 23, no. 1 (February 2010).

38. Barth, of course, would not have claimed otherwise. Nevertheless, there are moments when he writes of the grace of God-in-Christ in terms so triumphant that it overwhelms his human creatures' distinct and relatively self-determining existence.

yields freedom to the beloved; and third, my reading of the opening chapter of the book of Genesis, where God, making humankind in his own image, yields creative and discretionary freedom to Adam as to a vicegerent.

There are some forms of human good that do not require direct reference to God, for example, knowledge of the truth about subatomic physics or about the moral distinction between intentional and accidental killing. One does not need to acknowledge God to recognize that friendship and the experience of beauty belong to human flourishing. The phenomena of personal intimacy and a glorious sunset take away the breath of believers and nonbelievers alike. Of course, for a believer, communion with God is basic to human flourishing; but there is more to human flourishing than what is basic.

Whereas Barth's ethics tend to be too exclusively theological in practice, in principle he recognizes that common sense and nontheological reflection can yield material for a Christian ethic, and that Scripture and theology are not its sole sources.[39] Thus he endorses Luther's description of Hammurabi as "an exponent of the order of God."[40] He praises the Greeks for grasping in their concept of *eros* the fact that real, flourishing human being is "free, radically open, willing, spontaneous, joyful, cheerful and gregarious."[41] He acknowledges that Rousseau had theoretical and practical insights about politics that have an affinity with his own views of Christian political thought and action.[42] He credits Kant with expressing "the essential concern of Christian ethics" by pointing out that the concept of what is pleasing or useful cannot of itself produce the concept of what is obligatory, and he approves of Kant's definition of the ethical as that which may be expressed in terms of a universal law.[43]

In principle, then, Barth allows theological ethics to "be absolutely

39. See Biggar, *Hastening That Waits,* chap. 5, "Eavesdropping in the World."

40. *Karl Barth's Table Talk,* ed. John D. Godsey, Scottish Journal of Theology Occasional Papers, no. 10 (Edinburgh: Oliver and Boyd, 1963), p. 75.

41. Karl Barth, *Church Dogmatics,* ed. G. W. Bromiley and T. F. Torrance, vol. 3, *The Doctrine of Creation,* pt. 2, trans. Harold Knight et al. (Edinburgh: T. & T. Clark, 1960), p. 283.

42. Barth, "The Christian Community and the Civil Community," pp. 180-81.

43. Barth, *Church Dogmatics,* II/2, pp. 650, 656.

open to all that it can learn from general human ethical inquiry and re-ply," for "finally and properly its own Whence? and Whither? are not alien to any philosophic moralist." This openness, however, is not un-critical, as is indicated by the aggressive Old Testament metaphor that Barth uses to describe the way theological ethics relates to its nontheological counterparts: "annexation." Theological ethics may adopt and use and operate in terms of ethical material from outside theology, but only by "annexing" it, taking it over, incorporating it into a dominantly theological system, and modifying it accordingly: "Annex-ation remains annexation, however legal it may be, and there must be no armistice with the peoples of Canaan and their culture and cultus."[44]

In Barth's case, some excuse for the discrepancy between openness in theory and theological exclusivity in practice might be found in the methodological distinction that he makes between "theological ethics" and "Christian ethics." The role of theological ethics is to derive basic ethical principles from dogmatics, whereas the "actual handling of the problems of human life" in the light of those principles is the specific business of Christian ethics.[45] It is not entirely clear that Barth consis-tently thought himself to be doing only the former, but even if it were clear, his methodological self-limitation would still be problematic for two reasons.[46] First, the formulation of ethical principles is not separa-ble from the moral analysis of cases. The relationship is not one-way, from the top downward. Casuistical analysis is not merely a matter of "applying" ready-made principles. On the contrary, the very meaning of principles is informed by reflection on concrete cases. As Kenneth Kirk puts it: "Every . . . principle is partially illuminated by the known in-stances in which it holds good; without such known instances it would remain a mere unmeaning formula. . . ."[47] Principles or rules are forms of shorthand: we know what they mean only insofar as we assume cer-tain paradigmatic cases. So, for example, I understand the rule that pro-

44. Barth, *Church Dogmatics*, II/2, p. 524.

45. Barth, *Church Dogmatics*, II/2, p. 542.

46. Biggar, *Hastening That Waits*, p. 159.

47. K. E. Kirk, *Conscience and its Problems: An Introduction to Casuistry* (London: Longmans, Green, 1927), p. 107.

hibits murder, because I have in my mind certain classic cases that tell me what murder is. Thus the traffic between principles and cases is two-way — up as well as down. Casuistry is dialectical.[48] What this means is that the business of deriving ethical concepts from theological affirmations is not independent of the business of working out the normative meaning of those concepts with respect to human conduct in concrete cases. To observe a division of labor between theological ethics and applied Christian ethics is to weaken both.

The second objection is this: if the theologian confines himself to only half of the ethical task — deriving ethics from dogmatics — who exactly, does he imagine, will complete the rest? Christians who are legislators, government ministers, civil servants, managers, and pastors generally have less time for reflection than academics; and the ethical interpretation of the concrete problems of human life is often a far from simple matter. Why should professional moral theologians grant themselves the luxury of an indeterminacy that the rest of humanity can ill afford?

To insist that a Christian ethic needs to work dialectically from both ends at the same time — to think back and forth between the dogmatic and the casuistic — is not to say that it should commit itself unreservedly to a particular casuistic judgment. Oliver O'Donovan is correct to warn that the Christian ethicist's concrete moral pronouncements should be modestly hypothetical: "[U]seful recommendations will tend to be introduced by the useful word 'if.'" After all, these depend on what the ethicist knows about the facts of the case; and that will certainly be limited and probably inexpert. Ethicists who reflect on medical practice, the social responsibility of the media, and foreign policy will have some knowledge of medicine, journalism, and international relations; but they will not have the same level of expertise as do physicians, journalists, and diplomats. And besides, the interpretation of empirical data is seldom beyond dispute. Nevertheless, I cannot quite agree with O'Donovan's statement that

---

48. For more on "dialectical casuistry," see Nigel Biggar, "Moral Reason in History: An Essay in Defence of Casuistry," in *Issues in Faith and History,* Scottish Bulletin of Evangelical Theology, Special Study 3 (Edinburgh: Rutherford House, 1989); Biggar, "A Case for Casuistry in the Church," pp. 42-44; and Biggar, *Hastening That Waits,* pp. 40-41.

"[a]ny private contribution to a current political debate . . . is not . . . in a position to offer precise recommendations."[49] On the contrary, I think that some energy needs to be conserved for emphasizing the ethicist's duty to have enough courage to take the risk of venturing precise judgments, albeit ones that do not pretend to be final or conclusive. The reason for this is that people in positions of institutional or governmental leadership carry responsibility (sometimes onerous) for making decisions (sometimes momentous) under pressure of limited time. Therefore, it is incumbent on those of us who have ethical expertise to take moral principles and to show what they might amount to concretely in a range of relevant hypothetical cases.[50] This furnishes "the burden-bearers of the world" — to use Reinhold Niebuhr's sympathetic phrase — with models of moral reasoning against which to hone their own deliberation efficiently in the light of the actual circumstances in which they find themselves.[51] Not to venture precise hypothetical judgments, it seems to me, is to leave the ethical task only half done. And I think it unfair to expect laypeople to have the leisure to finish the job.

The integrity of Christian ethics, therefore, does not demand that the moral theologian limit himself to the squeezing of dogmatic tenets for the juice of ethical concepts, leaving to others the task of figuring out how these generic or specific concepts should bear on concrete conduct and issue in particular judgments. Nor does it insist on the eschewal of conceptual abstraction and analysis for the drawing of

49. Oliver O'Donovan, *The Just War Revisited* (Cambridge: Cambridge University Press, 2003), p. 127. I note that here O'Donovan contradicts William Temple, who argues, in *Christianity and the Social Order* (New York: Penguin, 1942), that whereas the church as a corporate body should deal only in the currency of general principles, individual churchmen may offer casuistic counsel in a private capacity (pp. 18-19).

50. I find myself arguing here along lines very similar to those of Ronald Preston, who held that there are occasions when the church should take the risk of making precise judgments about policy ("Appendix 2: Middle Axioms in Christian Social Ethics," in *Church and Society in the Late Twentieth Century: The Economic and Political Task* [London: SCM, 1983], pp. 153-54), but that it would have been better if, instead of simply proposing one particular course of action, *The Church and the Bomb: Nuclear Weapons and the Christian Conscience* (London: Hodder and Stoughton, 1982) had "listed other feasible ones, with arguments for and against each" ("Appendix 2," p. 151).

51. See, e.g., Reinhold Niebuhr, *An Interpretation of Christian Ethics* (New York: Seabury, 1979), p. 15.

analogies directly from the text of the New Testament. Nor does it require the assumption that theology always touches on every important point of moral argument, and that what it does not touch is by that token unimportant. No, what the integrity of Christian ethics requires is careful reflection, running all the way up and down the chain of moral reasoning between the theologically sublime and the casuistically meticulous, on whether the ethical concepts used are sufficiently shaped at all the appropriate points by relevant moments in the whole theological narrative. In a nutshell: granted creedal completeness, what we need is not distinctiveness but discrimination.

CHAPTER 2

Tense Consensus

It is important that Christian ethics maintain its theological narrative integrity. Self-respect requires it; for if Christian ethics were to cut itself adrift from its theological moorings, then it would no longer be itself and would have to change its name. Social responsibility also requires it; for theological premises will sometimes press the Christian ethicist to say something important that no one else is saying. Sometimes the voice of Christian ethics will be distinctive, and should it fail to speak, society would be so much the poorer.

On the other hand, distinctiveness is not everything. Indeed, it is strictly beside the point. Sometimes what the Christian ethicist says will not stand out; sometimes it will merely echo what others are already saying. But maybe that is not so mere, after all. Over twenty years ago I complained in print about a report published under the auspices of the Church of England's Board for Social Responsibility that it permitted the church only "to proclaim more loudly the good that the world already knows, but not the good that comes to the world as news."[1] While I still think that the target of that remark deserved it, it now occurs to me that there might be merit in adding one's voice to a chorus. Indeed, if the chorus is declaring the truth, then there surely is merit in it. What is good and right deserves the church's support, and the fact that others are already speaking up for it is no good reason for

1. Nigel Biggar, "Any News of the Social Good?" A review of *Changing Britain*, *Theology* 91, no. 744 (November 1988): 496.

the church to keep its mouth shut — as if the only role worth playing were that of solitary prophet in sole possession of the heroic limelight. If the church attracts allies, or finds itself facing an opportunity to become one, then that is surely cause for rejoicing, not sulking. After all, the church exists for the sake of the good of the world that God so loves, not for the sake of displaying its own indispensability (which is not to say that it isn't indispensable).[2]

Besides, theological narrative integrity itself should lead the Christian church to expect to find common ground with others. The Christian ethicist has good theological reasons to expect that unbelievers will not feel the need to deny everything that he affirms. The very first moment in the theological narrative is the moment when God creates the world. This God is one, undivided and unrivaled, and his creation reflects this sovereign unity in its own coherent order. The creating God is also benevolent, repeatedly confirming (according to the first creation "myth" in the book of Genesis) that what he has created is not only ordered but good. Since the created world is ordered, it is therefore comprehensible by rational creatures, especially humans, who reflect God's image. And since the created world is ordered for good, what is comprehensible includes goods or forms of flourishing.

The second major moment in the theological narrative, however, is the Fall, whereby human creatures are alienated from their Creator. As a consequence, their regard for themselves and for others becomes distorted by hubris, and when hubris overreaches itself, then by anxiety or despair. This false self-estimation — now excessive, now deficient — in turn distorts their rational grasp of human goods and their practical requirements (that is, norms of behavior). In principle, it could be that the effect of this condition of religious alienation, or "sin," has been to distort moral understanding so completely that sinful humans can have no accurate grasp of goods or moral norms *at all,* and thus that

2. The theologically vigilant will retort, "But surely the church exists primarily for *God's* sake!" Yes, it does, but not if God's sake is supposed to be an alternative to the world's. We are, after all, talking about the God who chose to characterize himself in terms of the world-loving Jesus. So whatever serves this God *ipso facto* serves the good of the world. The First Epistle of John puts the point sharply: "If anyone says, 'I love God,' yet hates his brother, he is a liar" (1 John 4:20).

those who have been saved from sin have nothing ethical in common with them, and nothing ethical to learn from them. It could be so; but there are cogent empirical, biblical, and theological reasons to suppose not.

First of all, it is not at all an uncommon experience of Christians to find that nonbelievers share (some of) their own ethical views. Christians are not the only ones to believe in human dignity, for example, or in the virtue of justice, or that murder is wrong. Christian pacifists find that they are not without non-Christian allies, as do Christian just-war proponents.[3]

The Bible itself reflects this common experience. The Wisdom literature of the Old Testament, for example, borrows liberally from ethical cultures other than Israel's — not least that of Egypt — and the Pastoral Epistles of the New Testament baptize lists of virtues conventional in Greek and Roman society.

Christian theology adds two reasons why Christians should expect to find a grasp of moral truth outside the walls of the church, one ecclesiological, the other soteriological. The first is that it is not clear to human perception who belongs to the people of God and who does not. The boundary between those who profess to belong and those who profess not to belong is obvious enough. But the Gospels are clear in saying that this obvious boundary is not the last word. Not everyone who professes to be a follower of Jesus really is one (Matt. 7:21-23), and any puritan attempt to weed the wheat field will have the evil effect of uprooting some wheat (Matt. 13:24-30). Jesus' own career should give pause to any Christian who presumes to think that moral understanding and insight is the monopoly of the church, for was not Jesus himself judged morally heterodox by the "God's people" of his day? Any genuine Christian disciple, then, will be ready to hear the voice of the Spirit coming from unexpected quarters.

Further, if Christians consider themselves to have been saved from sin, they consider themselves at the same time to be in the *pro-*

---

3. James Gustafson makes the further point — equally true — that believers sometimes find that nonbelievers possess superior moral virtue and wisdom (*Can Ethics Be Christian?* [Chicago: University of Chicago Press, 1975], pp. 1-2, 22, 80).

cess of being saved from it. On the one hand, Christians believe that God in Christ has taken the initiative to overcome the alienation that is sin. This he does partly through the unilateral volunteering of compassion for creatures who do evil either without recognizing it (Luke 23:34) or under the impulsion of perplexing forces whose self-destructiveness — and so irrationality — they know all too well (Rom. 7:14-23). This divine initiative of grace has happened and is given, and it constitutes the basic moment of salvation, which is complete and constant and may always be relied on. Christian life stands on it and lives out of it by faith. On the other hand, the subsequent process of moral growth is not complete. Christians who live out of faith in God's gracious love still have the task of letting their nascent penitence, humility, faith, and hope ramify intellectually and behaviorally. They have much to do in recovering their moral understanding and their embodiment of that understanding from the distortions of sin. They remain not only imperfect, but corrupt. If they are, in a certain sense, already *iusti,* then they are also still *peccatores.* What this means is that, even if all who profess themselves Christian were "saved," they would nevertheless share with "unsaved" non-Christians a common need for the enlightenment and correction of moral understanding — and for the growth of moral character. Therefore, Christians should certainly not presume that they have nothing to learn. And since they have reason to suppose that the church is not the only place where true moral words are spoken, they should bend a humble and docile ear to what is said outside of it.

Notwithstanding an entirely proper concern for theological narrative integrity — and to some extent precisely because of it — the Christian ethicist should expect to find common ethical ground with others. Although sin undoubtedly clouds human apprehension of the moral order that inheres in the world of the one God's creating, its obfuscation outside the church is evidently not absolute. And its de facto sphere of influence inside the church has not yet been brought to an end. So Christians have good empirical, biblical, and theological reasons to listen to what others say about what is good and right.

Most Christian ethics acknowledges this, one way or another, and to a greater or lesser extent. In the thirteenth century the seminal Thomas

Aquinas incorporated a concept of "natural law" into his theological ethic, according to which the grounds and norms of moral obligation are built into human nature, where they are objectively available to human intellectual grasp — in principle. In fact, however, human understanding is more or less corrupted by sin, and it therefore needs the therapeutic aid of what is revealed in Scripture in order to see straight. Notwithstanding this qualification, it is clear that, for Aquinas, human reason unaided by special revelation is still capable of grasping accurately some important ethical things, as is implied by his own heavy borrowing from the ethical thought of the pre-Christian Aristotle.

After the Reformation, Thomist thought about natural law came to dominate Roman Catholic moral theology; but it also continued to influence Anglican moral thinking through Richard Hooker, whose *Laws of Ecclesiastical Polity* (c. 1554-1600) expresses a high estimation of the power of natural reason to perceive our moral duties (as distinct from the requirements of salvation). In addition, the reach of (Thomist) natural law thinking extended into some Lutheran ethics through Philipp Melanchthon,[4] who was more inclined than Luther himself to affirm human understanding's continued possession, after the Fall, of "natural light."[5] In his *Loci Communes* (1521), for example, he says that natural law is the "common knowledge to which all people agree in the same way, to the extent that God implanted it into the heart of each of us with the intention of forming morals" (p. 22). The Fall weakens our power to

4. While Melanchthon agreed with Luther that obedience to the law is not the route to salvific justification, he nevertheless reckoned that those who have been justified need the moral guidance that law can provide; and in true Scholastic fashion he believed that the content of that law, although present in the Old and New Testaments, is best discovered through natural reasoning (see, for example, *Epitome philosophiae moralis,* 1541). It is not clear that Melanchthon ever read Aquinas for himself. He did receive a Scholastic education at Tübingen, and while it is true that by his time the *via moderna* as well as the (Thomist) *via antiqua* were being taught there, Aquinas's approach to the natural law was followed by almost every Scholastic theologian after Abelard (according to Jean Porter in *Natural and Divine Law* [Notre Dame, IN: Notre Dame University Press, 1999]). Whatever the truth of the provenance of Melanchthon's thought, it is quite clear that he shares with Aquinas the belief that reason is still capable of grasping the natural law, notwithstanding the effects of sin.

5. See Charlotte Methuen, *Science and Theology in the Reformation: Studies in Theological Interpretation and Astronomical Observation in 16th-Century Germany* (Edinburgh: T. & T. Clark, 2008), p. 12. Hereafter, page references to this work appear in parentheses in the text.

do what is right more than it weakens our intellectual grasp of it (p. 24). It is true that Lutheran and Reformed ethics have generally tended to have a dimmer view of the postlapsarian capabilities of human reason than did Aquinas, Hooker, and Melanchthon;[6] and it is true that they have thus taken their ethical cue from the Old and New Testaments rather than from observation of, or reflection upon, "nature." Nevertheless, Luther himself acknowledged that moral philosophy is competent in matters ethical and civil (p. 10). Both he and Calvin acknowledged the natural politico-ethical wisdom of the pagan Greeks and Romans, and appealed to natural law when treating political matters.[7] And, as we have already seen,[8] even Karl Barth, who is a rare Protestant rival to Luther in his suspicion of what passes for "reason" and whose brisk rejection of Thomist "natural law" is infamous, still found something to praise in the ethics of Hammurabi, the Greeks, Rousseau, and Kant.[9]

The concept of a moral law that is somehow given in the nature of things — especially the nature of human being — and which is somewhat graspable by human reason, despite the wounds of sin and apart from what has been revealed through Scripture, is the way in which most Christian ethics have made sense of the evident fact that moral insight is not the preserve of members of the Christian church. Not that this is simply a reluctant bending of theology to a facet of reality that

6. See Methuen, *Science and Theology,* ch. 2, "Natural Order or Order of Nature? Natural and Moral Philosophy in the Thought of the Reformers," where Methuen makes clear the difference between Melanchthon, on the one hand, and Luther, Zwingli, and Calvin, on the other; and ch. 3, "*Lex naturae* and *ordo naturae* in the Thought of Philip Melanchthon," esp. p. 30, where she affirms Melanchthon's close approximation to Aquinas.

7. John T. McNeill, "Natural Law in the Teaching of the Reformers," *Journal of Religion* 26 (1946): 168-82.

8. See chap. 1 above, p. 19.

9. Karl Barth, *Church Dogmatics,* ed. G. W. Bromiley and T. F. Torrance, vol. 3, *The Doctrine of Creation,* pt. 4, trans. A. T. MacKay et al. (Edinburgh: T. & T. Clark, 1961), p. 22; Karl Barth, *A Letter to Great Britain from Switzerland,* trans. E. H. Gordon (London: Sheldon Press, 1941), p. 17; Barth, "The Christian Community and the Civil Community," in *Community, State and Church,* ed. Will Herberg, trans. A. M. Hall et al. (Gloucester, MA: Peter Smith, 1968), pp. 163-64; Nigel Biggar, *The Hastening That Waits: Karl Barth's Ethics,* rev. ed. (Oxford: Clarendon Press, 1995), pp. 52-56; and "Karl Barth and Germain Grisez: An Ecumenical *Rapprochement,*" in *The Revival of Natural Law: Philosophical, Theological, and Ethical Responses to the Finnis-Grisez School,* ed. Nigel Biggar and Rufus Black (Aldershot: Ashgate, 2000), pp. 165-66.

can no longer be denied. As I have argued above, there are plenty of internal reasons why theology should bend willingly.

I need to be clear, however, about what I mean in affirming natural law, and what I do not mean. What I mean is that sinful human creatures not only can, but do have *some* grasp of the principles of morality — that is, without the aid of Scripture's witness. What are these principles? Most basic are the goods, which together comprise what it means to flourish as a human being — for example, physical life and friendship. More specific are the behavioral norms generated by the intrinsic value of these goods: for example, the virtues of respect for another's life and faithfulness to him, and the action-obligations not to murder him or lie to him. Sinful humans might also discern correctly what these generic obligations require in concrete circumstances: for example, whether the duty not to murder forbids a doctor knowingly to administer a probably lethal dosage of morphine to a suffering and terminally ill patient, or whether the duty not to lie requires a householder to give an affirmative answer to the Gestapo's question, "Are there any Jews hiding in your attic?"

From the empirical fact of this common access to valid moral understanding, however, some exponents of natural law wrongly infer the independence of ethics from the Christian theological narrative and conclude that there is no such thing as a specifically Christian ethic. Take, for example, the Danish Lutheran Knud Løgstrup, whose work is currently enjoying a revival of interest.[10] Løgstrup argues that Jesus' proclamation is religious only "in a very general and vague sense."[11] It

10. Løgstrup's *The Ethical Demand* was first published in Danish in 1957, and then in German and English, in 1959 and 1971 respectively. The University of Notre Dame Press republished it in 1997. In 2007, Notre Dame published a collection of essays by Løgstrup himself (*Beyond the Ethical Demand,* ed. Kees van Kooten Niekerk, trans. Susan Dew, Heidi Flegal, and George Pattison [Notre Dame, IN: University of Notre Dame Press, 2007]), and a collection of essays by others on his work (*Concern for the Other: Perspectives on the Ethics of K. E. Løgstrup,* ed. Svend Andersen and Kees van Kooten Niekerk [Notre Dame, IN: University of Notre Dame Press, 2007]).

11. Knud Ejler Løgstrup, *The Ethical Demand,* intro. Hans Fink and Alasdair MacIntyre, trans. Theodor I. Jensen, Gary Puckering, and Eric Watkins (Notre Dame, IN: University of Notre Dame Press, 1997), p. 3. Hereafter, page references to this work appear in parentheses in the text.

31

can surprise us by disclosing something of which we were hitherto unaware. However, for a disclosure to be intelligible, it must "answer to . . . features of our existence" and therefore be graspable "in strictly human terms" (p. 2). The ethical sum of what Jesus discloses is that "the point of God's demand is that in his reflections a person takes as his point of departure not his own well-defined interests but that which serves the other person's welfare" (p. 111). By implication, the ethical demand for such radical selflessness (p. 105) is a constant feature of human existence — part of its *nature* — which is "there" for human grasping, and which Jesus merely illuminates and draws our attention to. Beyond this, according to Løgstrup, Jesus' proclamation is silent, containing "no directions, no rules, no morality, no casuistry . . . nothing which relieves us of responsibility by solving in advance the conflicts into which the demand places us" (p. 109). To spell out the demand in detail would be to objectify it, to make it a purely external matter "with no thought given to our own relation to it," to absolutize it (pp. 110-12) and thus to encourage the notion that "[e]verything can be carried out quite mechanically; all that is needed is a purely technical calculation" (p. 114). From this it follows that, when it comes to specifying the normative content of the ethical imperative,

> the Christian must make decisions on exactly the same bases as those upon which anyone else decides. The person to whom the Christian message is the decisive truth about existence will not find in this message specific Christian arguments for any particular view of marriage, child-rearing, the purpose of punishment, or the political or economic structure of society. They must support their view of these matters like everyone else, using arguments which make sense to non-Christians as well as Christians. . . . Christianity does not endow a person with superior political or ethical knowledge. (p. 111)

Svend Andersen encapsulates Løgstrup's position thus: "Christian faith does not imply its own ethic. The ethic of neighbour-love is a universal ethic, which is entirely intelligible in human terms." Andersen proceeds to strengthen the cogency of the second sentence of his summary statement by qualifying the first in terms of Luther himself.[12] Therefore, the Christian is characterized by two kinds of righteousness. The first, *iustitia aliena,* is the property of Christ, in which we share by grace through faith. The second, *iustitia propria,* is our own, but only in the sense that we exercise it in cooperation with — on the basis of, under the influence of — the first. Christian ethics is not exactly identical to neighbor-love (and this is Andersen's qualification) because *iustitia propria* contains three elements: regarding the self of the still sinful believer, the mortification of concupiscence; regarding others, neighbor-love; and regarding God, humility and fear. Self-mortification is closely bound up with neighbor-love in that seeking the best for the neighbor involves selflessness, even self-sacrifice. Nevertheless, the normative form *(die Struktur)* of neighbor-love is adequately expressed in the Golden Rule, which is a summary of natural law and its common moral insight. As Luther says: "Nature teaches how love should behave: that I should do as I would be done by."[13] What this implies, according to Andersen, is that non-Christians possess a knowledge of right conduct, which somewhat agrees with the basic principles of Christians' neighbor-love *(das eine gewisse Übereinstimmung mit der Gesinnung der Nächstenliebe hat);* and that this makes possible consensus between them on temporal matters *(im Bereich des Weltlichen).*[14]

It is important to note that Andersen does not entirely agree with Løgstrup. While he shares a belief in the possibility of consensus between Christians and non-Christians, and does so on the basis of "a certain agreement" *(eine gewisse Übereinstimmung)* between the Golden

---

12. Svend Andersen, "Die Rolle theologischer Argumentation in öffentlichen Leben," in *Religion und Theologie im öffentlichen Diskurs: hermeneutische und ethische Perspektiven,* ed. Gotlind Ulshöfer, Arnoldshainer Texte, Bd 132 (Frankfurt am Main: Haag und Herchen Verlag, 2005), p. 11-18: "[D]er christliche Glaube gar keine Ethik impliziert. Die Ethik der Nächstenliebe ist eine allgemeine, auch rein human verständliche Ethik."

13. Quoted by Andersen in "Die Rolle theologischer Argumentation," p. 17: "Die Natur lehrt, wie es auch die Liebe tut: dass ich tun solle, was ich mir selber getan wissen wollte."

14. Andersen, "Die Rolle," p. 17. If James Gustafson's account is accurate, then Andersen's position is typically Lutheran *(Can Ethics Be Christian?* pp. 151-53).

Rule and neighbor-love, he respectfully dissents from Løgstrup's "thesis of the non-existence of a Christian ethic."[15] This is because he holds, with Luther, that there is more to that ethic than norms of action; there are also norms of disposition — that is, virtues. Further, there are normative dispositions toward God and the self, as well as toward the human neighbor. So Christian ethics comprises more than the Golden Rule that one should do as one would be done to, and more than a disposition of love for the neighbor. It also involves a normative disposition toward God and a correlative disposition toward the self. However, while these Christian dispositions enable the sinner to love her neighbor by selflessly seeking the best for him, they do not affect that love's normative active form, which is satisfactorily expressed in the Golden Rule. In other words, in this view, what the Christian theological narrative adds to natural law is a certain view of the self and corresponding virtues and motivation. It makes no difference, however, to the norm of action. This is how we should understand Andersen when he remarks that, during his membership of the Ethical Council of Denmark, "not once was my theological background decisive."[16] Here he is at one with Løgstrup.

To this view I have three objections. The first takes issue with Løgstrup's assumption that, in order to be intelligible, the ethical content of Jesus' proclamation must be expressible "in strictly human [as opposed to theological] terms." Such an assumption is practically atheistic in its implication that relationship with God is not a natural feature of human existence. Theistic Christians are bound to assume the contrary and thus to expect Jesus' proclamation to illumine the nature of human existence in such a way as to show that theological reference is needed to do it full justice.

Next, it simply is not true that the specification of the ethical demand in terms of norms of action must reduce moral life to a matter of external conformity and technical calculation. There is no logical or practical reason why an ethic cannot develop specific action-norms

15. Andersen, "Die Rolle," p. 17: "Løgstrups These über die Nichtexistenz einer christlichen Ethik. . . ."

16. Andersen, "Die Rolle," p. 10: "Nicht einmal mein theologischer Hintergrund war entscheidend."

while acknowledging that such development is never beyond doubt, controversy, and revision, and while recognizing the importance of virtues, motives, and intentions.

Third, I doubt that neighbor-love and the Golden Rule are universally recognized as norms of action. There are, after all, actual egoists, some of them philosophically principled, many more of them brazenly opportunistic. However, even if neighbor-love and the Golden Rule were universally recognized norms, I doubt very much that the Christian theological narrative would make no difference to their content. The Golden Rule itself structures the relationship between lover and beloved in terms of equality, such that reciprocity may be expected. What it does not determine is who is my equal, from whom I may expect reciprocal behavior. That is, it leaves open the decisive question: *Who* is my neighbor? Is a Samaritan or a Gentile? Is a black Briton or American, a Pakistani or a Latino, an Arab or a Jew, or a hindered human adult who is not "rational" in the sense of being capable of self-direction, or a human fetus, or a dolphin? Nor does it tell me whether near neighbors are to be preferred to distant ones.

Then there is the question of the nature of the good. The Golden Rule would have me govern my treatment of others in terms of how I myself would wish to be treated. Ultimately, I need to articulate my rationale for the latter in terms of an understanding of human good or flourishing. But that is highly controversial. We disagree about what goods comprise this flourishing — about whether, for example, communion with God is among them. We disagree about whether we can rank these goods rationally — and if so, how. We disagree about whether we may intentionally damage some goods for the sake of others — and if so, under what conditions. Consensus about the duty to love one's neighbor in a manner structured by the Golden Rule covers a multitude of conflicting material interpretations, of which an ethic informed by the Christian theological narrative is one. The fact that Svend Andersen found nothing to dissent from in the deliberations of the Ethical Council of Denmark need not mean that his theological background made no material difference. It could mean, of course, that he had not perceived how theology should have made a difference. Or, more charitably, it could mean that he enjoyed the good fortune of finding himself among colleagues who were all Kantian humanists. Had they been utilitarian disciples of Peter Singer or antihumanist disciples of John Gray, however, his experience would have been very different. At least, I hope it would.

The Lutheran Løgstrup-Andersen view of natural law and Christian ethics finds an almost exact echo in the school of "autonomy-ethics" that emerged in Roman Catholic circles in the 1970s. Reacting against positivist, heteronomous, and excessively theological versions of a *Glaubensethik*[17] — an ethic directly and distinctively specified by Christian faith — and keen to develop opportunities for constructive dialogue with nonreligious humanists, Josef Fuchs, Bruno Schüller, Gerard Hughes, Richard McCormick, and others argued for the autonomy of ethics.[18]

I agree with their opposition, but not with their proposition. Ethics may be autonomous in the sense that each individual must exercise her conscience as best she can; but it is not autonomous in the sense that individual conscience has nothing to learn from Christian theological tradition. To start with, while an unaided, autonomous grasp of human good and what it requires is possible in principle, the fact of sin can often prevent it from being achieved in practice. The more we specify an obligation, the more demanding it becomes; and the more

17. Thus Bruno Schüller, SJ, complained that "contemporary Catholic theology . . . seems to be distancing itself more and more from philosophy and thinks it can say something pristinely theological on every conceivable topic" (Schüller, "A Contribution to the Theological Discussion of Natural Law," in *Natural Law and Theology*, ed. Charles Curran and Richard McCormick, SJ, Readings in Moral Theology, no. 7 [New York: Paulist Press, 1991], p. 87).

18. See Vincent MacNamara, *Faith and Ethics: Recent Roman Catholicism* (Washington, DC: Georgetown University Press, 1985), pp. 37-55. More particularly, see Josef Fuchs, SJ, "Is there a Specifically Christian Morality?" in *The Distinctiveness of Christian Ethics*, ed. Charles Curran and Richard McCormick, SJ, Readings in Moral Theology, no. 2 (New York: Paulist Press, 1980), pp. 3-19; Bruno Schüller, SJ, "The Debate on the Specific Character of Christian Ethics: Some Remarks," in Curran and McCormick, *Distinctiveness*, pp. 207-33; Schüller, "A Contribution to the Theological Discussion of Natural Law," in Curran and McCormick, *Natural Law*, pp. 72-98; Gerard Hughes, SJ, "The Authority of Christian Tradition and of Natural Law," in Curran and McCormick, *Natural Law*, pp. 17-42; and Richard McCormick, SJ, "Does Religious Faith Add to Ethical Perception?" in Curran and McCormick, *Distinctiveness*, pp. 156-73.

demanding it becomes, the less inclined a sinful agent will be to acknowledge it. The vice of cowardice (in the face of prevailing social prejudice), fortified by the vice of (nationalist) self-righteousness, for example, might move the agent to deny that this African or this Armenian or this Jew or this Tutsi is a member of the human family at all, and that to kill her is to do murder. Sinful humans, therefore, have a sufficient grasp of moral principles to be held responsible for offending against them; and they may sometimes also discern accurately what these principles require concretely. On other occasions, however, the unpalatable nature of these requirements will rouse selfish rationalization to deflect them by distorting their import. Sin distorts moral cognition as well as moral motivation. This, I take it, is part of what Thomas Aquinas meant when he wrote that concupiscence or some other passion can both hinder the decent application of a known general principle to a particular case and obscure derivative principles altogether.[19] So that is one reason why I do not think that the affirmation of natural law should be taken to imply that ethics are "autonomous." The ethical traditions of the Bible and Christianity involve the salutary restatement of ethical truths that are often obscured by sinful rationalization.

However, that is not all; for Christian theological narrative also reveals ethically important truths that are not available at all to "natural reason" — that is, to human apprehension of the moral order that is given in the nature of things. For example, the claim that God is at work in history to save his creation and bring it to fulfillment engenders hope, prevents demoralization, and fuels moral resilience. It also helps human beings accept the limits of their own creaturely power and exercise patience toward the inevitable compromises of secular justice. The Christian narrative, therefore, grounds certain virtues and fuels moral motivation in ways that the created moral order alone does not, and that other narratives need not.

In the course of their debate with the champions of the *Glaubensethik,* the autonomy-ethicists agreed that Christian faith does add a religious supercontext to ethics, foster certain virtues, raise moral am-

---

19. Thomas Aquinas, *Summa Theologiae,* Ia IIae, q. 77, a. 2; q. 94, a.6.

bition, and fuel moral motivation. However, they tended to deny that it makes any difference to material norms of behavior.[20] I think that this is a mistake.[21] After all, virtues are material norms, too. Beyond this, however, I think that the biblical witness to salvation history not only restates obscured moral truths, not only grounds fresh virtues, and not only fuels motivation — it also prescribes new norms of action, new duties of conduct. It adds an understanding of how we should behave if we are to respect and serve goods under the conditions of sin and in the light of God's salvific action. It shows us how to act at once rightly and salvifically. This salvific ethic involves, for example, certain remedial religious or spiritual practices — such as prayer and worship — that are designed to reverse our alienation from God, and to foster the virtues of penitence, humility, faith, and hope. And religious practices are not something separate from Christian ethics.[22] They are part and parcel of what, from a Christian point of view, human beings need to do in order to flourish — and hence *should* do. Further, following the pattern of God's salvific, atoning initiative in Jesus, the revealed salvific ethic also involves a certain way of responding to the injuries that other sinners cause: namely, through "forgiveness" in the forms of forbearance and compassion and a will to reconciliation. These are elements of moral duty that will not make sense — or will not make *as much* sense — to human reason apart from the theological narrative revealed in Scripture, and crucially in the life, death, and resurrection of Jesus.

Germain Grisez offers a more satisfactory account of natural law

---

20. Josef Fuchs is a rare exception. In addition to arguing that there is a specifically Christian "intentionality" and motivation, and that there are specifically Christian "transcendental attitudes and norms," he also admits that these sometimes issue in specifically Christian "categorical ways of conduct" — for example, the practice of virginity and religious and cultic conduct ("Is There a Specifically Christian Morality?" pp. 5-6, 14-16).

21. So does Vincent MacNamara in his fine analysis of the debate between the proponents of the *Glaubensethik* and the autonomy-ethicists (*Faith and Ethics,* pp. 117-18, 163, 202).

22. To the Protestant eye of this author, it seems that the autonomy-ethicists' tendency to regard ethics as independent of salvific revelation is reflective of an unfortunately persistent Neo-Scholastic distinction between nature and the supernatural, the moral and the spiritual.

than do the autonomists.[23] On the one hand, in the first volume of his elaborate and comprehensive system of moral theology, *Christian Moral Principles,* Grisez expounds the basic human goods before introducing the themes of sin and redemption. Thereby he gives the impression that the goods can be understood — accurately, if not completely — through reason alone, unaided by reference to the biblical story of salvation. This impression is confirmed when he tells us that one can come to know the goods by rational reflection on the *experience* of "privations which mutilate them" (in the case of existential goods),[24] and on the *experience* of natural or spontaneous inclinations toward them (in the case of substantive goods) (7.D.4).

This initial impression, however, is removed by further reading of *Christian Moral Principles.* We are told that in the light of revelation "natural law is *restored,* completed, and elevated. . ." (7.B.8; italics added). The words "completed" and "elevated" are consistent with our initial impression: reason can grasp a body of moral knowledge (the natural law) that may need supplementation, but that is nevertheless sound in itself. However, the word "restored" implies something significantly different: that reason's knowledge is not only incomplete but defective and — in some respects, at least — unsound.

The nature of this defect becomes clearer when Grisez explains how he thinks Christian revelation transforms our understanding of the principles that specify what makes our pursuit of human flourishing reasonable.[25] Apart from special revelation, he tells us, "no widely accepted morality is free of gaps, misunderstandings, and false norms"; and these defects appear especially "in dealing with moral evil and its consequences, and in interacting with individuals and groups beyond one's own clan, tribe, caste, or nation" (25.E.11). This is be-

23. What now follows, concerning Grisez, is a mildly revised version of part of my chapter entitled "Karl Barth and Germain Grisez," in *The Revival of Natural Law,* pp. 176-79.

24. Germain Grisez, *The Way of the Lord Jesus,* vol. 1, *Christian Moral Principles* (Chicago: Franciscan Herald Press, 1983), 5.D.7. Hereafter, page references to this work appear in parentheses in the text.

25. That is, the "modes of responsibility" or the primary specifications of the first principle of morality ("will those and only those possibilities whose willing is compatible with a will toward integrated human fulfillment") (7.E, F, G). For the Christian transformation of these, see Grisez, *Christian Moral Principles,* 26: "Modes of Christian Response."

cause the fallen human condition is one characterized by sin, whose species include: lack of confidence that action for good will be efficacious (26.D.1; F.1; I.1; K.1); fear of pain, suffering, and death (26.G.1; F.1); lack of trust in other people (26.E.1; I.1); partiality toward one's own people (26.H.1); and the resentful pursuit of vengeful "justice" against wrongdoers (J.1). In these various forms, sin undermines "an upright and energetic pursuit of human goods" and causes us to be "constantly tempted to deal with evil inappropriately — for example, by destructive methods or renunciation of human hope for a good life in this world" (27.A.4). What Christian revelation does is read the human condition as at once fallen and redeemed (25, Summary [p. 617]). Christian moral life, then, is distinctively characterized by its holding in tension both realism and hope (25.E.13).[26] On the one hand, Christians may not overlook the fact of wrongdoing or evil; and they must expect to suffer on account of it (26.G, K). On the other hand, the Resurrection of Jesus gives them reason to hope that integral human fulfillment — that is, the simultaneous flourishing of all human beings together — is possible beyond this life by the grace of God (7.F.2; 19, Intro.; 27.A.3), and that therefore unswerving commitment to the human good — and especially friendship with God — is not futile (22, Summary [p. 544]; 21.D.8). Such hope then fuels in each Christian the patient and strenuous following of his or her personal vocation (26.F.1; G.1; I.1), the acceptance of a limited role for oneself in the world's redemption (26.E), respect for others as equal subjects of a personal calling (26.H),[27] the will not to resort to evil means of combating evil (21.D.8; 26.J.1, K.1; 27.A.4-6; 28.G.6), and thus the eschewal of vengeance for conciliation (26.J).

The defect that revelation remedies, then, is partly one of moral motivation. What sin — or lack of faith in God — does is undermine

26. 25.E.13: "The distinctiveness of Christian morality is clearest in its linking together seeming opposites. For example, one must love enemies, but absolutely refuse to compromise with them; one must suffer for the sake of uprightness, but not passively regard the world as broken beyond human repair; one must concede nothing to anyone's moral error, yet judge no one wicked."

27. Grisez himself does not quite establish the (psycho)logical connection between accepting one's own role in the world's redemption as a limited one, respecting the roles of others, and treating them with compassion and generosity.

commitment to the claims of practical reasonableness, leading people into inertia; into impatient individualism; into "tribalism";[28] into action driven by the myopic desire for a particular satisfaction, by the frantic desire for immediate satisfaction, by the fear of pain and death, or by resentment; and into compromising with evil. Part of what is lacking in those who live without revelation and faith is the power to behave as they know they should.

That, however, is not all. The defect from which human moral agents suffer apart from revelation and faith is not just volitional but also cognitive. For example, while they recognize the good of human life, they define too narrowly who possesses it. And while they recognize the good of justice, they mistake the action it obliges as the wreaking of vengeance on wrongdoers.

So far, so good. Even so, I think that Grisez still underestimates the extent to which moral reason is shaped by its metanarrative hinterland. This is because those who lack faith in God, and thus lack hope in the possibility of the postmortem achievement of integral human fulfillment, will not see the requirements of Grisez's version of "practical reasonableness" *as reasonable.* It will not make as much sense to them that they should eschew consequentialist or utilitarian reasoning. The spuriousness of attempts to calculate the greatest aggregate good will not be so obvious. And the norm of action that one should never intend to destroy some instances of the good of human life for the sake of saving or improving others will not seem rational. In a world where there appears to be no God and no hope for integral fulfillment beyond this life, the requirements of Grisez's "practical reasonableness" seem *unreasonably* restrictive. The implication of this is that the presence or absence of theological faith and hope can determine what seems morally "reasonable," and that Grisez's account of natural law, even at the level of normative action, is in fact more shaped by the Christian salvation narrative than he himself recognizes.

To affirm natural law, then, should be to affirm the following: that there is a form of flourishing that is given in and with the nature of human being; that reflection on human nature can achieve an under-

---

28. The term is mine, not Grisez's.

standing of that flourishing and its component basic goods; that reflection on human experience can produce a grasp of kinds of disposition and action that respect and promote those goods; that all human beings are, despite their sinfulness, *somewhat* capable of an accurate grasp of basic goods and their practical requirements; and that, therefore, there are sometimes areas of ethical agreement between Christians and others. None of this, however, makes the Christian theological salvation-narrative ethically irrelevant. It does not say that sinful humans have the motivation to do sufficiently what they know to be right, apart from the penitence, faith, gratitude, and hope that the story of God's salvific initiative inspires. Nor does it say that they have the power, unaided by biblical tradition, to know completely what is good, what is virtuous, or what is right.[29]

This implies that the nature of ethical agreement between Christians and others is properly Augustinian rather than Rawlsian. According to the explicit thought of the late John Rawls, different "comprehensive doctrines" (that is, worldviews or metanarratives) can support a common "overlapping consensus" about the nature of human being and its ethical requirements. While this consensus about "public reason" is arrived at by a variety of routes, according to Rawls, its content floats free of its various origins. In the face of this, however, the account of natural law that I have just espoused raises a skeptical eyebrow, for it holds that ethics are deeply informed by their metanarrative hinterland. And Rawls himself confirms the doubt when he admits that the overlapping consensus contains controversy that sometimes must be decided by majority vote.[30] He fails to ask, however, what it is that gives

29. I am pleased to note that, as it happens, the median line that I have pursued in the first two chapters of this book reiterates that taken by my doctoral mentor, Jim Gustafston, in 1975: "Two extreme types of positions are possible. One is that Christian principles of action are always defensible on rational moral grounds; the 'Christian' and the 'rational moral' are convertible. The other is that to be a Christian is to follow a certain moral way of life decisively, primarily or even exclusively because of a special calling to be followers of Jesus. . . . I have attempted to make a case that fits neither extreme" (*Can Ethics Be Christian?* pp. 167-68).

30. I argue this point exegetically in "Not Translation, but Conversation: Theology in the Public Debate about Euthanasia," in *Religious Voices in Public Places,* ed. Nigel Biggar and Linda Hogan (Oxford: Oxford University Press, 2009), pp. 178, 183-84.

rise to dissensus within the agreed terms of the consensus. Neverthe-less, he implies the answer when he discusses the issue of public policy about abortion, where he observes that the interpretation of public rea-son made by the Roman Catholic Cardinal Bernardin differs from his own (Kantian) one.[31] The implicit answer to the question of the prove-nance of dissensus is that, while the various metanarratives do support a generic consensus, at the same time they also structure differing spe-cific interpretations of it.

The nature of ethical agreement between Christians and others is not Rawlsian, but Augustinian. It is not whole and stable, but partial and provisional. Augustine acknowledges that members of the city of God share with members of the earthly city a common interest in tem-poral goods — above all, justice — and a sufficiently common reading of them to permit a measure of public agreement. At the same time, he is clear that without love for God there is no true or perfect justice. What this implies is that, insofar as Christians agree with non-Christians, they should regard it as an imperfect compromise, subject to criticism and yearning for perfection.[32]

So, yes, consensus — but tense.

31. See John Rawls, "The Idea of Public Reason Revisited," in *The Law of Peoples* (Cambridge, MA: Harvard University Press, 1999), pp. 169-71.

32. How to read Augustine on this matter is, of course, controversial. In a 1970 essay, "*Ordinata est res publica:* The Foundations of Political Authority," R. A. Markus offers a liberal reading of Augustine's concept of "the secular" as neutral, autonomous space (Markus, *Saeculum: History and Society in the Theology of St. Augustine* [Cambridge: Cam-bridge University Press, 1970], pp. 72-104). In *Theology and Social Theory: Beyond Secular Reason* (Oxford: Blackwell, 1990), John Milbank opts for an antiliberal reading, in which justice that is not qualified by love for God is not merely imperfect but no justice at all (p. 406). More recently, Markus has moved his position to the right of his original stance but to the left of Milbank: absent love for God, justice is less than perfect but more than just apparent (Markus, *Christianity and the Secular* [Notre Dame, IN: University of Notre Dame Press, 2006]). This seems to me to make coherent sense of both of Augustine's views: that agreement between members of the city of God and the earthly city *is* possible; but that without love for God, justice is not "true." This, then, is what I present as the Au-gustinian position.

CHAPTER 3

Which Public?

On the one hand, Christians should look to the integrity of their ethics — to its theological narrative integrity — albeit with a blithe disregard for the accident of its distinctiveness. On the other hand, they should expect to find consensus with non-Christians over ethical matters — but only occasionally and provisionally. What does this imply for the proper nature of Christian participation in public deliberation about ethical matters? In order to answer this question, we must first consider what we should mean by "public." That is the task of this chapter.

Etymologically, the word "public" designates "the people as a whole" or what concerns it.[1] "The public," therefore, refers to a community. What is public is what is common to a community. But it is more than that, for "public" is not an exact synonym for "common." More specifically, it refers to the formal affirmation of something as common law, policy, or property by a legal or political authority.

There are, of course, many communities, each having its own people and its own public arrangements. Accordingly, in Oxford University, "public examinations" are those conducted by the authority of the university as a whole, not of any constituent college. The fact that these examinations are "public" does not mean that they are open to just anyone; only members of the university may take them. Similarly, debate in

1. According to the *New Oxford Dictionary of English* (Oxford: Oxford University Press, 1998), "public" derives from the Latin *publicus,* which is a blend of *poplicus* ("of the people," from the Latin *populus,* or "people") and *pubes* ("adult").

the General Synod of the Church of England may be called "public" without its being open to anyone but official members. The word "public," then, almost invariably refers to the common concerns of a particular institution or definite people. I say "almost invariably" because some institutions and peoples are more comprehensive than others; and one might be maximally capacious. Presumably, a universally representative global assembly would be "public" in an unrestricted sense.

The publics that will concern us here are those that involve both Christians and non-Christians, that is, almost any public other than that of a church or a body of churches. This could be the public of a school or university, of a business or a charity, of a local or national or international body; and the forum for public deliberation could be a school committee or a board of management, a town council or a national parliament or an international assembly, local radio or the BBC World Service. I will call these publics "secular" — in the Augustinian sense of "plural," not in the sense of "religion-free."[2]

This choice of focus does not imply that ecclesial publics and forums are of no consequence. Not at all. The public good of Christian churches is important, too. Indeed, for the Christian ethicist, the proper well-being of churches will have a certain priority. After all, the most direct, graphic, and effective witness to the light of God in Christ will be the lives of those who daily live by it, the social structures they build, and the public policies they enact — not the lectures and tomes of teachers and scholars of ethics. The national public is largely shaped by civil social publics, including churches and families, in which individuals are primarily formed as individuals-in-society.[3] So if Christian

2. In contemporary colloquial speech, "secular" means "religion-free." For Augustine, however, "secular" referred to the *saeculum,* or the "age" between the Resurrection and the eschaton, when Christians and pagans, the righteous and the unrighteous, the saved and the damned must live alongside each other and negotiate a common life. In Augustinian terms, then, "secular" refers to what is ambiguous, plural, and provisional.

3. I derived this particular point from a reading of Reinhard Hütter, "The Church as Public: Dogma, Practice, and the Holy Spirit," *Pro Ecclesia* (Summer 1994): 349, 352-53, where he argues against what he calls "modernity's foundational dichotomy between private and public" (p. 349). While I doubt that there is a single (Worldly) system called "modernity," to which the private/public dichotomy is fundamental, I recognize that much contemporary liberal discourse does assume wrongly that there is such a thing as a "pri-

ethicists would play a part in that witness, they should be concerned to shape the lives of churches and their members directly, and to promote their public good.[4]

Nevertheless, an important part of the witness of the churches consists in what they say when they address non-Christians in nonecclesial forums about public matters, and in the manner of their saying it. Most Christians live most of their lives working, playing, and talking with people outside of the church — with the exception, perhaps, of some clergy. So it is actually not beside the point of shaping ecclesial life for Christian ethicists to reflect on the proper nature of Christian participation in secular public deliberation. For such participation is bound to be a large part of the life of the churches, whenever they dwell in societies that are not entirely composed of Christians — which nowadays means almost always.

Beyond this, it will belong to the vocation of the Christian ethicist to make direct contributions to secular debate about public goods. This is so for several reasons. First, it should matter to the Christian ethicist whether a secular institution or society shapes itself for good or ill, because accordingly it will shape its members. He might believe that there is more to human well-being than material and social goods, but he will not believe that there is less. He might believe that the final salvation of the world will involve the radical transformation of instances of temporal goods, but he will not suppose it to amount to their simple annihilation.[5] After all, while the resurrected Jesus was so changed as to be difficult to recognize, he was nonetheless still *Jesus.*[6] Christians who would

---

vate" realm that can be neatly separated from the "public" realm. I also accept what Hütter reports of scholarship that shows that Saint Paul's ecclesiology transgressed the ancient (not-so-modern, then?) dichotomy between the polis and the *oikos* (pp. 352-53).

4. By "Christian ethicist," I mean any Christian with expertise in ethical reflection, analysis, and reasoning, not just those who occupy posts in moral theology at institutions of higher learning.

5. Here I depend on N. T. Wright's interpretation of the apocalyptic genre in the New Testament. Its talk of the destruction of the old world and its replacement by a new one, according to Wright, should not be taken to mean the annihilation of the former. Rather, it should be read as a dramatic, hyperbolic way of indicating the astonishingly radical nature of its transformation. See Tom Wright, *Who Was Jesus?* (London: SPCK, 1992), pp. 54-56.

6. According to the Gospels, the disciples experienced some difficulty in recognizing the risen Jesus: e.g., Luke 24:13-35, John 20:11-18. In his First Letter to the Corinthians

bear witness to the God-who-so-loved-the-world-in-Christ are bound to care for that world's good *as such,* and in all its aspects, even the contingent ones.

Second, the Christian ethicist's expertise will mean that he is better equipped than most other members of secular society to analyze ethical issues, and better equipped than most other members of the churches to articulate a Christian view of them. Therefore, he owes it both to society at large and to the churches to put his skills to public service.

And third, as a *Christian* ethicist, he will be keen to demonstrate in secular public forums how friendship with God is important for human and social well-being, and thus why it matters. Therefore, his contributions to public deliberation will be at once ethical arguments and exercises in Christian theological witness.

For several reasons, then, it is quite appropriate for us to reflect on the proper nature of Christian contributions to deliberation about ethical issues in secular public forums. Having established that, we can now proceed to ask whether and how the nature of these forums should play a role in determining what a proper Christian intervention is. The publics that concern us here are "secular" ones; that is, they comprise non-Christians as well as Christians, agnostics and atheists as well as religious believers. This means that the Christian contributor to public deliberation will be addressing some people who do not share all or any of his theological premises. It is often assumed that a majority of his interlocutors will be "nonreligious," for whom theology is simply unintelligible, and that therefore he should at least suppress his theology, or even argue on sufficiently nontheological grounds. That is, it is commonly asserted that religious believers should adopt "secular" language in public.

This prescription usually rides on the back of the secularization thesis. It assumes that religion is inexorably on the wane, and that in "modern" societies adherents of theological beliefs are, and always will be, a minority. Secular publics in the modern world are thus not just composed of peoples with a plurality of points of view; they are predom-

---

(15:35-57), Paul reflects on the nature of post-Resurrection existence in terms of a "spiritual body." Insofar as it is spiritual, it is significantly different from the physical, pre-Resurrection existence; but insofar as it is bodily, it is the same.

inantly nonreligious. Such, for example, is the view of Jürgen Habermas, the eminent German philosopher and European public intellectual.[7] Despite expressing a greater appreciation for the moral resources of religion, and a correlative anxiety over what is being lost through its waning, Habermas persisted, in public addresses and interviews between 2000 and 2002, in seeing secularization as inevitable. "Modernization," he says, largely fueled by scientific progress, leads to "detraditionalization"; and since "the buffers of [religious] traditions have, in the course of these processes, been nearly exhausted," "modern societies have to rely on their own secular resources for regenerating the energies that ensure their own moral cohesion."[8] Habermas takes it for granted that contemporary Western societies are "modern," and that they are thus "secular" in the sense of being predominantly and teleologically nonreligious. Therefore, a bias appears in his vision of public deliberation. He argues that in complex societies one culture can convince a majority through succeeding generations of "the advantages of its world-disclosive semantic and action-orienting potential," and it may hence prescribe for minorities a country's common political culture.[9] In the modern West, the dominant culture is secular. Therefore, the religious minority has to make itself understood to the "secular majority" (but not, it seems, vice versa).[10] Translation is one-way: from religious statements into "secular" language.

To be fair, Habermas qualifies this bias by enjoining the "secular"

7. What follows here, concerning Habermas, is a slightly revised version of parts of my essay entitled "Not Translation, but Conversation: Theology in Debate about Euthanasia," in *Religious Voices in Public Places*, ed. Nigel Biggar and Linda Hogan (Oxford: Oxford University Press, 2009), pp. 166-70, 171-72. My reading of Habermas on religion in public discourse differs from that of Maureen Junker-Kenny in that same volume ("Between Postsecular Society and the Neutral State: Religion as a Resource for Public Reason," in Biggar and Hogan, *Religious Voices*, pp. 58-81).

8. Jürgen Habermas, "The Debate on the Ethical Self-Understanding of the Species," in *The Future of Human Nature*, trans. William Rehg, Max Pensky, and Hella Beister (Cambridge: Polity, 2003), p. 26. This essay was first delivered as an address on June 28, 2001.

9. Jürgen Habermas, "Are there Postmetaphysical Answers to the Question: What is the Good Life?" in *The Future of Human Nature*, pp. 2-3. This essay was first delivered as an address on September 9, 2000.

10. Habermas, "Faith and Knowledge," in *The Future of Human Nature*, p. 109. This essay was first delivered as an address on October 14, 2001.

side to remain "sensitive to the force of articulation inherent in religious languages" during the search for reasons "that aim at universal acceptability." And in one passage he goes so far as to recognize that "the boundaries between secular and religious reasons are fluid," and to urge that "[d]etermining these disputed boundaries should therefore be seen as a cooperative task which requires *both* sides to take on the perspective of the other one."[11] Nevertheless, the bias continues to resurface: in an interview published in *Le Monde* in December 2002, Habermas still argues that, since views presented in religious rhetoric cannot count on democratic assent, "*the* task" is to "translate their message into public languages that are universally accessible — for example, into a philosophical language."[12]

Habermas's views on these matters have continued to develop: two of his more recent[13] writings manifest greater sympathy for the point of view of religious believers. I refer to "Vorpolitische Grundlagen des demokratischen Rechtsstaates?" first published in October 2004, and "Religion in der Öffentlichkeit," first published in 2005. In these writings Habermas insists on symmetry in the moral burdens that public discourse imposes on believers and unbelievers.[14] There should be a "two-way learning process" *(einer doppelter Lernprozess),* in which both the traditions of the Enlightenment and religious traditions reflect on their own limits.[15] Fairness requires *all* citizens, secular as well as reli-

---

11. Habermas, "Faith and Knowledge," p. 109.

12. Habermas, "Habermas entre démocratie et génétique," *Le Monde* 20 (Décembre 2002): 8: "Il est vrai que les opinions présentées au moyen d'une rhétorique religieuse ne peuvent compter sur l'assentiment démocratique que si elles sont traduites dans un langage universellement accessible, par example un langage philosophique. . . . Entrepris dans un ésprit qui ne vise nullement à critiquer les réligions, le travail consistent à traduire leur message dans les langages publics et universellement accessibles serait l'exemple d'une sécularisation qui sauve au lieu d'anéantir." The italics in the translation have been added.

13. Relative, of course, to the time of my writing (August 2008).

14. Habermas, "Religion in der Öffentlichkeit," in Jürgen Habermas, *Zwischen Naturalismus und Religion: Philosophische Aufsätze* (Frankfurt am Main: Suhrkamp, 2005), pp. 137-38. Since the time of my writing, this volume has been translated and published in English as *Between Naturalism and Religion: Philosophical Essays* (Cambridge: Polity Press, 2008).

15. Habermas, "Vorpolitische Grundlagen des demokratischen Rechtsstaates?" in *Zwischen Naturalismus und Religion,* p. 107.

gious, to adopt the perspectives of others.[16] "Philosophy" needs not only to acknowledge the phenomenon of the persistence of religion as a bare social fact, but also to take it seriously as a cognitive challenge.[17] Religiously "unmusical" citizens should stop viewing religious convictions as "quintessentially irrational" *(schlechthin irrational)*,[18] and should open themselves to the possible truth-content in them.[19] Moreover, religious citizens should not be forced to put their devout existence at stake by dividing themselves into private and public personae, and offering only secular translations when acting in the latter role. They should be allowed to contribute to public deliberation in their own theological language (pp. 132-34, 136).

This permission of theological reasons, however, only applies to the informal political public forum. In public institutions such as the legislature, legislative elections, the judiciary, government, and the civil service, only secular reasons should count. Why? Because the exercise of (state) power *(Herrschaftsausübung)* must be neutral with regard to worldviews (p. 136), lest their persistent rivalry cause political community to disintegrate into an unstable *modus vivendi* (pp. 141-42). Therefore, while religious citizens should not be compelled to translate their theological reasons into secular ones fit for deployment in the formal political public forum, they should be expected to understand how their own religious convictions appear to nonbelievers — "reflexively, from outside" — and to appreciate the need to find secular equivalents (p. 136). That is, they should recognize the "institutional translation proviso" *(diesen "institutionellen Übersetzungsvorbehalt")*. And if religious citizens themselves are not able to offer a translation, then they should help their nonreligious fellows do it for them (p. 136).[20]

At first glance, this last suggestion seems reasonable enough. On closer inspection, however, it first becomes puzzling — and then turns

16. Habermas, "Religion in der Öffentlichkeit," in *Zwischen Naturalismus und Religion,* pp. 125-26.

17. Habermas, "Vorpolitische Grundlagen," p. 113.

18. Habermas, "Vorpolitische Grundlagen," p. 118.

19. Habermas, "Religion in Öffentlichkeit," p. 138; see also pp. 145, 149. Hereafter, page references to this essay appear in parentheses in the text.

20. This is the best sense that I can make of Habermas's talk of "cooperative achievements of translation" *(die kooperativen Übersetzungsleistungen)*.

suspect. For if religious citizens are unable to translate theological statements into secular ones, how can they still cooperate with their nonreligious fellows in producing translations? If genuine translation is not possible, then no one can do it and there's nothing to cooperate in. So what Habermas implies is that genuine translation is possible but that religious citizens lack the wit to perform it themselves. Indeed, Habermas says as much when he says that "many citizens, who express their opinion on political questions from a religious point of view, are simply not sufficiently knowledgeable or imaginative to come up with secular grounds that are independent of their own convictions . . ." (p. 132).[21] Accordingly, cooperation is possible in that, once secular citizens take the lead, their religious peers can follow in an auxiliary capacity. Here, it seems to me, Habermas's expanded sympathy for religious citizens strikes a rather illiberal, patronizing note, echoing the typical Enlightenment view that modern philosophy is needed to rescue essential moral concepts from primitive and superfluous religious myth.

This lapse into modernist prejudice is not an isolated instance. It surfaces again when Habermas refers to "religious certainties of faith" (in contrast to "fallible convictions of a secular nature"); describes them as subject to increasing pressure to engage in (critical) self-reflection *(einem zunehmenden Reflexionsdruck);* complains that they withhold themselves from "unreserved discursive discussion" by appealing to "the dogmatic authority of an inviolable core of infallible truths of revelation" (p. 135); and fears rule by a religious majority that would impose its will without due respect for the democratic principle that all decisions enforceable by the state "must be capable of justification in language that is equally accessible to all citizens," and refuses the minority "the discursive comprehension of the justifications due to it" *(den diskursiven Nachvollzug der ihr geschuldeten Rechtfertigungen)* (p. 140).

Let us grant that some forms of religion are authoritarian, incapable of honest conversation, and repressive. Let us also grant that the influence of such religion could pose a serious threat to a liberal society

21. In the original this reads: ". . . dass viele Bürger, die aus religiöser Sicht zu politischen Fragen Stellung nehmen, gar nicht kenntnis- und einfallsreich genug sind, um dafür säkulare, von ihren authentischen Überzeugungen unabhängige Begründung zu finden."

and to social peace. Nevertheless, why does Habermas write as if authoritarian tendencies are peculiarly religious? Has he forgotten about Marxist authoritarianism so quickly? Is he unaware of dogmatic, antireligious secularism? Has he never come across a religious believer who acknowledged that he might be mistaken? Does he himself not adhere to dogmas (say, that human life does not inhabit a moral void) that he can barely rationalize, but that he would be very loath indeed to surrender?[22] Notwithstanding genuine growth in his sympathy for the religious point of view, it seems to me that Habermas still adheres to modernist prejudice.

Habermas's views raise three questions about the nature of secular publics. The first concerns the sociological claim — which he was making at least as late as December 2002 — that these are predominantly nonreligious. The second is about his prescription of "secular" translation on the grounds of respect or fairness. And the third regards this prescription on the grounds of neutrality and political stability.

Habermas insists on the eventual translation of religious terms into secular ones in formal public forums, such as the legislature, legislative elections, the judiciary, government, and the civil service. I say "eventual" because he allows that theological reasons can be adduced in the course of debate, provided they are translated into secular ones in the end. One reason for this requirement is political-prudential: given that Western electorates are predominantly "secular" (i.e., nonreligious), religious rhetoric cannot count on winning democratic assent. However, the assumption that Western democracies are predominantly nonreligious is not now as plausible as when the secularization thesis reigned supreme. That is not now the case. Famously, of course, the United States remains predominantly and overtly religious. However, it is doubtful whether that assumption holds even for Europe. Britain is often held up as one of the most "secular" European countries, since so few of its population attend places of worship. A Tearfund survey of seven thousand adults throughout the United Kingdom in 2006 revealed that only 15 percent attend a Christian church at least once a month, with a further 10 percent attending somewhere be-

22. See Biggar, "Not Translation, but Conversation," pp. 165-66.

tween once a month and once a year.[23] Churchgoing in Britain is clearly the sport of a minority — sizable perhaps, but still a minority. On the other hand, 53 percent of those polled claimed affiliation with Christianity (and a further 6 percent with other religions); and there is reason to suppose that such claims express more than a merely nominal association.[24] The reason is this: the UK Government's Census of April 2001 returned a 71.6 percentile identifying themselves as Christian, which is a substantially larger proportion than that recorded by Tearfund.[25] Why the discrepancy? The Tearfund report offers the following explanation. The Census's question was "What is your religion?" whereas Tearfund's question was "Do you regard yourself as belonging to any particular religion?" Affirmative answers to the former included some from people who would have balked at confessing that they "belonged" to a religion, and whose affirmation was therefore arguably nominal. What this implies is that affirmative answers to Tearfund's question were expressive of a more substantial commitment.[26] Moreover, one cannot assume that nonchurchgoers are completely lacking in sympathy for religious beliefs. Had the 71 percent been positively hostile, it is unlikely that they would have described themselves as "Christian." Furthermore, of those Britons who reported in 2001 that they did not go to church, 41 percent nevertheless admitted to praying.[27] Further still, of those classified as "unreligious"

23. Jacinta Ashworth and Ian Farthing, *Churchgoing in the UK* (London: Tearfund, 2007), p. 6. These figures are very similar to those recorded by the 2004 British Social Attitudes Survey (p. 41).

24. Ashworth and Farthing, *Churchgoing in the UK*, p. 4. The 2008 British Social Attitudes survey records the similar figure of 50 percent identifying themselves as "belonging" to the Christian religion (Alison Park et al., eds., *British Social Attitudes: The 26th Report* [London: Sage, 2010], p. 67, Table 4.1).

25. Keith Robbins comments: "Given the supposed large-scale indifference and overwhelming rejection identified as being characteristic of society as a whole, the free decision of such a massive percentage [77 per cent owning a religious affiliation], 71.6 per cent of which registered as 'Christian,' is astonishing" (*England, Ireland, Scotland, Wales: The Christian Church, 1900-2000*, Oxford History of the Christian Church [Oxford: Oxford University Press, 2008], p. 471).

26. Ashworth and Farthing, *Churchgoing in the UK*, p. 4.

27. Ashworth and Farthing, *Churchgoing in the UK*, p. 1, citing the national poll of the Opinion Business Research, 2001.

by the 2008 British Social Attitudes survey,[28] 49 percent agreed that religion is beneficial in helping people find inner peace or happiness,[29] 42 percent scored 3-4 on a fourteen-point scale of religiosity, and only 3 percent scored zero.[30] According to other surveys, only a small minority of the population (15.5 percent) has positively declared itself to have no affiliation to any religion;[31] and a considerable majority (71 percent) has continued to claim to believe in a "God" of some kind.[32] It seems to me, therefore, that it cannot be presumed that a democratic majority of British people is impervious or hostile to religious discourse. And if this is true of the British, then it could also be true of the more churchgoing Germans and Dutch, not to mention the Spanish, the Austrians, the Italians, the Greeks, the Irish, and the Poles.[33] My

28. The Report on the 2008 British Social Attitudes survey contains a slight discrepancy. According to Table 4.6 (Park, *British Social Attitudes,* p. 71), 26 percent are "religious" (i.e., identify with a religion, believe in God, and attend services), 36 percent are "fuzzy faithful" (i.e., do two out of the three things that characterize the "religious"), and 31 percent are "unreligious" (i.e., do none of them). Later, however, these figures become 28 percent "religious," 39 percent "fuzzy faithful," and 33 percent "unreligious" (*British Social Attitudes,* p. 90). This is probably because the nonrespondents have been removed from the summary on p. 90.

29. Report on the 2008 British Social Attitudes, p. 72, Table 4.7.

30. Report on the 2008 British Social Attitudes, p. 92.

31. According to the UK Government's Census of April 2001. See www.statistics .gov.uk/cci/nugget.asp?id+293. The 2008 British Social Attitudes survey records only 18 percent of respondents saying that they "don't believe in God" at all (Park, *British Social Attitudes,* p. 68, Table 4.2).

32. See Grace Davie, *Religion in Britain since 1945: Believing Without Belonging* (Oxford: Blackwell, 1994), passim, but, e.g., p. 78, Table 5.1, and p. 2: "Why is it, for example, that the majority of British people — in common with many other Europeans — persist in believing (if only in an ordinary God), but see no need to participate with even minimal regularity in their religious institutions? Indeed most people in this country — whatever their denominational allegiance — express their religious sentiments by staying away from, rather than going to, their places of worship. On the other hand, relatively few British people have opted out of religion altogether: out and out atheists are rare." According to Table 5.1, a survey in 1990 showed that 71 percent of British people believe in "God" (p. 78). In *Europe: The Exceptional Case; Parameters of Faith in the Modern World* (London: Darton, Longman, and Todd, 2002), Davie cites a survey conducted ten years later (1999-2000). The percentage of British people who believe in "God" was virtually unchanged at 71.6 percent (p. 7).

33. According to the European Social Survey of 2002, in answer to the question "How often do you attend religious services except for special occasions?" 18.6 percent of Brit-

conclusion is that a genuinely *descriptive* sociology of Western democracies currently does not recommend, on grounds of prudence, a political rhetoric that suppresses theology as such.

What is true of a population as a whole might not be true, however,
of part of it; and that part might exercise a disproportionate influence
over the norms of public discourse. It appears, for example, that the
British media are hostile to politicians who confess religious belief in
public.[34] Tony Blair, for one, got his fingers badly burnt by admitting to
his religious convictions:

> It's difficult if you talk about religious faith in our political sys-
> tem. I mean if you are in the American political system or others
> then you can talk about religious faith and people say "Yes, that's
> fair enough" and it is something they respond to quite natu-
> rally. . . . You talk about it in our system and frankly people do
> think you're a nutter. I mean they sort of . . . [think that] you
> maybe go off and sit in the corner and you . . . commune with the
> man upstairs and then come back and say "Right, I've been told
> the answer and that's it."[35]

That is to say, "people assume that your religion makes you act, as a
leader, at the promptings of an inscrutable deity, free from reason
rather than in accordance with it."[36] The "people" whom Mr. Blair has
foremost in his mind here are journalists.

Some are inclined to find in Tony Blair's experience confirmation

---

ish respondents replied "at least once a month" — compared to 20.1 percent of Germans,
20.9 percent of Dutch, 28.9 percent of Spanish, 35.3 percent of Austrians, 44.1 percent of
Italians, 54.6 percent of Greeks, 67.2 percent of Irish, and 75.5 percent of Poles. See
Ashworth and Farthing, *Churchgoing in the UK*, p. 42.

34. See, for example, Mark D. Chapman, *Doing God: Religion and Public Policy in
Brown's Britain* (London: Darton, Longman, and Todd, 2008), pp. 9-16.

35. From the BBC documentary series, *The Blair Years*, whose first episode was origi-
nally broadcast on Sunday, November 18, 2007. This passage is quoted by Chapman in
Doing God, p. 14.

36. Tony Blair, "Faith and Globalisation," The Cardinal's Lectures 2008, Westminster Cathedral, London, April 3, 2008: http://tonyblairoffice.org/2008/04/speech-pn-faith-
globalisation.html; quoted by Chapman in *Doing God*, p. 15.

of the highly secularized character of British society. Thus the sociologist Callum Brown:

> Most Britons left their culture of Christian faith over the last forty years. . . . Their evacuation of this territory imparts to those who still occupy it, like Blair, an awareness that it [faith] can't be pushed too far. There would be a cultural incomprehension if it were. . . . In [this secularized] situation, no politician dare speak too much of the role of God in government.[37]

There are, however, two alternative interpretations. One is that British media institutions have developed a corporate bias against religion that is far less representative of wider society than they like to think. Institutions do develop corporate biases, and there is plausible evidence that this has happened, for instance, in the BBC.[38] Another interpretation is that Mr. Blair could have explained better how his religious beliefs and practices do, and do not, bear on political leadership. He could have made clearer, for example, that his praying to God about whether or not to go to war against Iraq did *not* mean that he was absolutely certain that the decision he eventually made bore the stamp of the Almighty. (If that had been his meaning, then those alarmed by it would have included hosts of religious believers, including this author.) As to what he did mean, his famous interview with Michael Parkinson on March 4, 2006, suggests that he was himself rather uncertain.[39] Perhaps there is a job here for an intelligible theologian to explain — after working it out — what exactly prayer is *for* in the process of decision-making.

Rhetorical prudence in societies that are supposed to be predominantly nonreligious is one of the reasons that Habermas urges the translation into secular language of religious contributions to public

37. Callum Brown, "'Best Not to Take it Too Far': How the British Cut Religion Down to Size": http://www.opendemocracy.net/globalization-aboutfaith/britain_religion_3335.jsp; quoted by Chapman in *Doing God,* p. 16. Chapman endorses Brown's interpretation.

38. See Robin Aitken, *Can We Trust the BBC?* (London: Continuum, 2007). Aitken worked for the BBC as a reporter and journalist for twenty-five years.

39. See Chapman, *Doing God,* pp. 10-12.

deliberation. Since that supposition is now open to doubt, so is the need for prudential translation.

A second reason is respect. It is supposed to be lacking in due respect for a religious believer to communicate with a nonbeliever in religious terms. This makes some sense, insofar as an interlocutor who refuses to recognize the different views of the person he is addressing fails to take that person seriously, treats her without due respect, does her an injustice. To make no attempt to persuade is to fail to recognize the other's difference; and to make no attempt to render one's own view in terms that the other might find acceptable is to fail to attempt to persuade. So religious believers who communicate with others exclusively in their own peculiar religious terms are behaving disrespectfully and unfairly. However, by the very same token, unbelievers who communicate with believers in relentlessly nonreligious terms are presumably also being disrespectful. So why is the burden of translation only placed on the shoulders of believers? Surely, in actual conversation, where due respect is paid, both parties will try to persuade each other by presenting their views in agreeable terms?

Note that what respect requires is not that we succeed in persuading others, but only that we sincerely *attempt* to persuade them. This point is Christopher Eberle's, and he makes it in his explanation of the "ideal of conscientious engagement."[40] Eberle is frank about the fact that, insofar as legislation is determined by majority vote, the defeated minority is bound to experience the resultant law as coercive (p. 50). That is, the infliction and suffering of coercion is a normal and unavoidable part of democratic politics. Nevertheless, the *way* that coercive legislation is decided is important: it is important that those who are coerced should be respected, and it is important for public peace that they should have good reason to feel respected (pp. 50, 65). Therefore, the religious citizen is obliged to exit his own parochial worldview, to inhabit the points of view of his nonreligious compatriots as far as she can, and "sincerely and conscientiously to pursue a widely convinc-

---

40. Christopher Eberle, *Religious Conviction in Liberal Politics* (Cambridge: Cambridge University Press, 2002), chaps. 4 and 5, esp. pp. 104-8. Hereafter, page references to this work appear in parentheses in the text.

ing secular rationale for his favored coercive laws." However, he is not obliged to succeed in his pursuit; and should he fail, then he is at moral liberty to support legislation on religious grounds alone (p. 10).

I almost agree with this, but not quite. It seems to me that any argument in a public forum is bound to articulate itself in terms of temporal public goods — such as national security or public health — since those are what public deliberation is, by definition, *about*. Therefore, insofar as it means talk about temporal public goods, "secular language" should always be used by religious citizens in public. Sometimes these citizens' religious beliefs will make no difference to their interpretation of goods, their ranking, and their practical implications; in that case, there will be no cause to invoke them. At other times, however, religious beliefs will make a difference, and it seems to me that on those occasions believers should not be required to suppress them — though rhetorical prudence might require careful thought about how, and when, to introduce them. I agree, then, that believers should respect nonbelievers sufficiently to strive to persuade them; and that successful persuasion involves the imaginative inhabiting of the other's point of view, and sensitive steering toward one's own. However, I am not convinced that respect requires an initial approach in which the religious person deliberately and systematically suppresses theological references.

The third reason that Habermas gives for insisting on "secular," nonreligious language in formal public forums is that the exercise of state power must be neutral with regard to worldviews, lest their persistent rivalry reduce political stability to a fragile, politically expedient *modus vivendi*. The differences here between Habermas and John Rawls are telling. First of all, Rawls talks of "public" reasons rather than "secular" ones, suggesting that these are reasons that are integral to some religious comprehensive doctrines, not alien to them. Public reasons belong to a definite overlapping consensus between certain religious and nonreligious worldviews. They are common rather than neutral. Second, Rawls acknowledges that public reason is not only common, but plural. Making up a consensus, it contains — that is, *limits* — controversy; but it also contains — that is, *includes* — controversy. Otherwise intractable standoffs between rival reasonable arguments, requiring decision by majority vote, would not arise as they do. He is clear that public reason contains room for disagreement — maybe subtle, but still significant — about how to understand the content of public goods, their ranking, and their moral implications. Nevertheless, it does seem that Rawls does not fully appreciate the extent and depth to which reasonable citizens can disagree.[41] More important, he does not seem to have grasped that this disagreement is generated by the operation of competing comprehensive doctrines *within public reason.* Had he done so, he would have come to see public reason not as a free-standing alternative to rival comprehensive doctrines, but rather as a shared anthropology and ethic of communication, which disciplines controversy between them.

If we give Rawls the benefit of the doubt and resolve his ambiguity in this direction, then we can say that public reason is not a neutral language that secures political stability by transcending the rivalry of comprehensive doctrines. Rather, it is a common (if thin) view of human being sufficient to generate a common set of communicative virtues and practices, which together govern the negotiation of persistent doctrinal rivalry. Read in this light, Rawls appears wiser than Habermas in his grasp of the nature of actual political debate and decision-making. He is more realistic about the ineradicable nature of doctrinal conflict, and thus about the need for public compromise and for minority forbearance in the face of majority triumph. He is also more to the point in implying that what political stability needs is not so much neutral language — as if such a thing were available — as the exercise of humane, liberal virtue. Not so much public reason, then, as public reasonableness.

What has all this taught us about whether and how the nature of the public should determine Christian contributions to it? First of all, public discourse should not be secular in the sense of "free of theological reference." Western peoples are not generally and predominantly nonreligious. Rather, they are plural, made up of some absolutely certain believers, some absolutely certain unbelievers, some who believe more than they do not, and some who do not believe more than they do. The members of Western publics are far more complex in their attitudes toward religion — and even more so toward spiritual realities — than the votaries of the secularization thesis allow. Political prudence, therefore,

---

41. Eberle agrees; see *Religious Conviction in Liberal Politics,* pp. 215-16.

does not demand that religious believers keep their public speech clear of theology.

Nor does respect for the dignity of those who think differently. Certainly, respect requires that I as a believer acknowledge the difference of unbelievers, that I engage with it, that I try to discern where we agree, in order to walk them from their point of view into mine. It requires that I reason with them reasonably. But respect for their atheistic difference does not require that I suppress my theistic one.

Nor does political stability require neutral public language. That is simply not to be had. Nor to be had is public space free of persistent conflict. We can have overlapping consensus and public reason. We can have common terms with a measure of common content. But consensus always contains dissensus. What we have in common, we hold differently.

So, *pace* Habermas and the explicit Rawls: public space should not be that from which theological references have been purged. Rather, it should be the plural place of polyglot negotiation and compromise over temporal, public goods, where tensions persist but are contained by a certain consensus about the ethics of communication and of handling disagreement.

This is "secular," but in the Augustinian sense of being a *modus convivendi* during the *saeculum* or the age between the Resurrection and the eschaton, when the wheat and the tares had best be allowed to grow alongside each other. On the other hand, since for Augustine there is no true justice apart from love for God, it follows that all secular agreements are subject to the judgment and the claim of that true justice that is only ever to be found in the eschatological city of God.[42] Members of the two "cities" may agree on certain goods, but they read them differently; and sometimes those different readings will lead to significant conflicts over the small print of law and policy.[43] In the *saeculum* we cannot expect public reason to iron out all the differences between worldviews. But we can hope that public reasonableness will contain them.

42. Augustine, *City of God*, XIX.17, 21.

43. It seems to me that Robert A. Markus's description of such peace as "autonomous" or "neutral" (*Christianity and the Secular* [Notre Dame, IN: University of Notre Dame Press, 2006], p. 40) tends to obscure this unsettled, still contested quality.

CHAPTER 4

Can a Theological Argument Behave?

Christians should look to the integrity of their ethics, and yet at the same time expect a measure of consensus with non-Christians over ethical matters. In the context of plural, polyglot, secular publics, Christians should want to say it as they see it — that is, theologically; and they should be allowed to. However, given the shameful history of bloody civil strife kindled by the misbehavior of religious believers, the question arises: Can Christians both speak authentically and responsibly in public?[1] Can their theological arguments *behave*? And if so, how?

The first thing to say is that theologico-ethical arguments come in different species, which vary in part according to the nature of their

---

1. I do not mean to endorse the popular modernist myth that religion is intrinsically and invariably violent, and has been *the* single most important cause of bloodshed in human history. The question of the causal relationship between religion and violence is a difficult one, requiring a complicated and nuanced answer, as David Martin has shown in general (*Does Christianity Cause War?* [Oxford: Oxford University Press, 1997]) and Philip Barnes has shown in the particular case of Northern Ireland ("Was the Northern Ireland Conflict Religious?" *Journal of Contemporary Religion* 20, no. 1 [2005]: 55-69). The Thirty Years War is one of the modernist myth-mongers' *loci classici* and is generally credited with inspiring secularist determination to liberate political life from the dangerous influence of religion. Yet in his recent exhaustive and highly praised history of that war, Peter H. Wilson argues that it was not primarily religious at all (*Europe's Tragedy: A History of the Thirty Years War* [London: Allen Lane, 2009], p. 9). Granted all this, history and current affairs are nevertheless all too generous in their supply of cases where religious believers have conducted themselves impatiently, intolerantly, and violently. Therefore, believers do need to take care to learn to behave.

public context. A Christian ethicist who is making an argument to a public made up of academic theologians, for example, will tend to frame that argument primarily in terms of a moral or political theological tradition. The reasons for this are several. In part, there may be the straightforward desire to demonstrate one's scholarly skills to one's academic peers. After all, commenting on classic texts is what real scholars (in the humanities) are supposed to do.

Then there might be the intention of showing one's loyalty to the theological tradition of one's own church. Roman Catholics will naturally refer to Thomas Aquinas, Lutherans to Luther, Presbyterians to Calvin, partly out of deference to the figures who dominate the thought-world of their respective traditions and partly to demonstrate their *bona fides* to their confreres.

Third, theologians tend to understand themselves as thinking out of a historical tradition, and so they want to articulate their views with reference to notable predecessors. This is not just the banal consequence of the fact that most theologians are members of particular religious communities with distinctive histories, though it is partly that. Nor need it be an ignoble expression of timid deference to classic authorities. On the contrary, it can be an admirable expression of an awareness — perhaps not so evident among moral philosophers of the analytic school — that the thought of finite creatures is bound up with their historical context; and it can also be an equally admirable expression of a determination to learn before one presumes to teach.

Fourth, Christian theologians understand themselves to be especially accountable to the witness of the Bible, upon whose veracity (at certain points) their central theological premises depend. Therefore, a moral theologian who is arguing about the ethics of sex is most likely to spend some time interpreting Genesis 1:26-28. Or if he is arguing about the ethics of the use of violent force, he will likely discuss the Sermon on the Mount and the thirteenth chapter of Paul's Epistle to the Romans. Or if he is arguing about the ethics of work, he might well refer to the book of Ecclesiastes.

Fifth — and most creatively — a moral theologian might want to come to grips with historical expressions of Christian thinking precisely in order to achieve intellectual liberation from the prison of common sense, and thus to develop a critical perspective on the present.

Finally, however, there is one less admirable motive: the desire to find in the classic texts of the tradition, not resources, but a refuge. There is a temperamental reason why many academics have chosen to spend their lives in the safety and seclusion of libraries rather than in the business boardroom, in the cabinet office, or on the battlefield. And academic theologians should be aware of their characteristic temperament and beware of the peculiar temptations it presents.

When addressing an ecclesia public, as distinct from an academic one, the Christian ethicist will probably feel the need to focus on addressing current concerns, if he is sensitive to his audience. Most of those listening to him will not be academics, and very few of them will have theological training. They may well have an intelligent interest, perhaps a very intelligent interest, in what Christians believe and why. But that interest is nonetheless likely to be oriented to the living of a faithful life — as a believer or a neighbor, as an adolescent or an octogenarian, as a mother or a husband, as a teacher or a streetsweeper, as a plumber or a manager, as a government minister or an office clerk. Most members of Christian churches are unlikely to have an interest in the history of theological thought for its own sake. And why should they? They will attend to classic texts insofar as they furnish insights that illuminate the practical issues that press upon them — but not otherwise. They will see texts as resources for living, not as ends in themselves, and so they should. So when the ethicist addresses church members, his main task should be to bring the fruits of his ventures into the tradition to bear more or less directly on their lives, rather than to make them retrace the laborious path by which he first discovered them. This is not to deny, of course, that from time to time he might decide to make his audience linger for a moment with John Chrysostom or *Rerum Novarum* or Karl Barth in order to introduce them to helpful resources for reflection, and perhaps also to reassure them that he is still committed to thinking *as a Christian.*

If this is true of the handling of theological tradition, is it also true of the Bible? When the Christian ethicist addresses an ecclesia audience, should his references to biblical texts be ancillary rather than primary? The answer depends on the brief. The New Testament contains the original witness to the historical Christ-event, on which the Christian church and its peculiar theological vision of things is founded.[2] The Old Testament furnishes the historical and intellectual background necessary to make sense of that event. Both Testaments together provide all the key moments that structure the whole Christian theological narrative. In that respect, then, the Bible is unlike theological tradition in that it contains the primary object of theological interpretation and the narrative in which it is located. All Christian theology is an interpretation of that object and its narrative, and is therefore beholden and subordinate to it. It is true, of course, that the New Testament does not give us the Christ-event in the pure form of naked fact. This always comes to us already bound up with interpretation. Still, all interpretation is by definition interpretation *of something given,* and the New Testament is no exception to this rule of logic.

So when a Christian ethicist addresses an ecclesial public, he will have reason in principle to refer to the New Testament in particular, and the Bible in general, more than he refers to the works of classic theologians. Still, whether he should refer to the basic, biblical terms of a Christian vision of things at all will depend on what his purpose is. If his task is to explain to an ecclesia audience how a characteristically Christian vision of reality bears on a particular moral question — say, the morality of voluntary euthanasia and its legalization — then he will be bound to advert to the fundamental biblical elements and structure of that vision. If, however, his aim is to explain why he judges voluntary euthanasia and its legalization to be morally right or wrong, then he may not think it relevant to advert directly, instead leaving hidden the indirect bearing of the Christian theological narrative on the matter.

Suppose, however, that a Christian ethicist is addressing a secular public — that is, one that is secular in the sense of being plural and polyglot. Should there be a place for biblical and theological references there? First no, then yes. First of all, there should be no place for *sheer*

2. When I speak of the "historical" Christ-event, I mean to say that this event happened in history, not that its veracity can be demonstrated by historical science, understood in a positivist way.

appeals to religious authority — be it the Bible or the Pope or the Qur'an.[3] This is not at all to say that one should never rely on an authority. Everyone does, and inevitably so. No one is able to confirm at first hand everything that she or he believes. Much of what each of us believes we take on trust from authorities — be they religious or scientific — to whom we give the benefit of doubt, and often with good reason. Nor do I mean to say that one should never appeal to authority. Such an appeal may well be appropriate while addressing fellow believers, who acknowledge it. In such a context, it might suffice to settle a point in dispute. Even among religious believers, however, appeals to authority are seldom beyond interpretative controversy, and they will often fail to satisfy unless supported by cogent argument.

To be sure, appealing baldly to a religious authority while addressing people who do not acknowledge it is both imprudent and disrespectful: imprudent because it is unlikely to impress or persuade; disrespectful because it fails to pay attention to the difference of the viewpoint of one's auditors. It refuses to engage with it, pushing past as if it were of no account, as if it were so stupid or wicked as to be beyond rational consideration. It refuses to concede that contradiction might have any ground at all. To dissenters, this is bound to seem insensitive and gauche, if not highhanded and insulting.

Therefore, there is no place for sheer appeals to religious authorities in secular publics (and probably not in religious ones either). But what about other kinds of biblical or theological reference? It might be that, in the course of making an ethical argument in public, a religious believer is moved to refer to a biblical story or saying — for example, the parable of the Good Samaritan or Jesus' saying that he who lives by the sword shall die by it. Would that be inappropriate? Not necessarily. It might be that such references serve to illustrate or illuminate an ethical point, or that they add persuasive force by drawing creatively on graphic or pithy material that, though religious, is still part of a polyglot society's common cultural stock. Their use could be rhetorically prudent.

---

3. By "sheer appeal" I mean the invocation of an authority to close down controversy, as in "The Bible says such and such; therefore, there is nothing further to discuss."

67

However, such references, though lodged in a religious tradition, are substantively ethical rather than theological, strictly speaking. They make no mention of God, his saving activity in the world, or of its eschatological fulfillment. More controversial and maybe more problematic, then, would be public references to theological beliefs, which are designed not just to illustrate or reinforce but to explain and justify. Take, for example, Karl Barth's appeal to God's self-revelation in Christ as a ground of the moral norm that all diplomacy should be open. This might very well baffle and alienate. But if it does, it is not because it involves a theological reference, but because it is at least an underdeveloped argument, and probably a bad one; and those alienated by it will include believers as well as nonbelievers. Not all Christian contributions to public discussion fall on ears made deaf by antireligious, secularist prejudice. Sometimes they deserve to suffer the fate of lead balloons, because they are poor arguments that are either underexplained or actually fallacious. Writing of the reception of Roman Catholic moral teaching, Jean Porter puts the point nicely:

> What can we [Catholics] say to convince men and women of good will who do not share our theological convictions or our allegiance to church teaching that early-stage embryos have exactly the same moral status as we and they do? It will not serve us to fall back at this point on blanket denunciations such as "the culture of death." Naturally, these tend to be conversation-stoppers. What is worse, they keep us from considering the possibility that others may not be convinced by what we are saying because what we are saying is — not convincing.[4]

Theological interventions, however, need not be denunciatory or logically careless. They need not bring public conversation to a rude and grinding halt. Suppose that a Christian ethicist is contributing to public discussion about how to deal with the violent legacy of a civil conflict. He urges the victims to display a measure of forgiveness by ap-

4. Jean Porter, "Is the Embryo a Person? Arguing with the Catholic Traditions," *Commonweal*, February 8, 2002, p. 8.

pealing to a duty of compassion. This he grounds in a certain duty of fairness, which conceives of the perpetrators as fellow creatures and fellow sinners. He then reinforces the rationality of forgiveness by invoking the theological hope that God will raise the murdered dead, and in that light acknowledges the empirical futility and counterproductiveness of vengeance. The concepts of creature and sinner, and more so, the concept of eschatological restoration, are theological concepts; and it is in these terms that a Christian naturally thinks. It is my view that a liberal, polyglot society should permit him to speak it as he sees it. But wouldn't this be rhetorically imprudent? Wouldn't nonbelievers be baffled by the theology and unpersuaded by it? Wouldn't it be a conversation-stopper?

Not necessarily. Others may not believe in God, but they may recognize in their own experience of the human condition something of the historical and social fatedness that creatureliness involves, and which codetermines wrongdoing along with individual choice. They may also recognize in their own experience some analogies between the wrongdoing that they have suffered and the wrongdoing that they have themselves inflicted. Christian talk about common creatureliness and sinfulness will not necessarily baffle nonbelievers. What they recognize, however, will more likely be the anthropological elements than the theological ones. They will recognize human limits and wrongdoing rather than common human responsibility to God, common human receipt of God's mercy, or common human hope for God's recovery of the lost at the end of time. This does not imply that the strictly theological elements are otiose. Not at all: they serve to reinforce the rationality of the forgiveness of enemies. What it does imply is that nonbelievers may grasp *some* of the good sense that the duty of forgiveness makes, without grasping it *all*.

Here we should recall that the actual world is not always divided starkly into believers and unbelievers, into Church and World. More often than not, it comprises a mélange of dogmatically certain believers, dogmatically certain unbelievers, and infinite gradations in between of more-or-less believers and more-or-less unbelievers. It is not only absolutely convinced believers who hope for God's recovery of the lost at the end of time, or those who believe more than they do not. Many who find it hard to believe that God exists nevertheless hope against their better judgment that he does, or at least hope for things that only a god could deliver. They hope strongly for the effect while remaining inarticulate about the cause. So when Christians make strictly theological references in the course of their public speech about forgiveness, for example, neither they nor anyone else is in a position to predict how much of what they say will baffle, how much will be half-grasped, or how much will be grasped with both hands. So let them speak it as they see it — and let the Spirit blow where it will.

Besides, insofar as a Christian's argument explains how a theological belief makes intelligible — or more intelligible, or optimally intelligible — a widely held moral principle or practice, it gives adherents of that principle or practice a reason to adopt the belief. A more-or-less unbeliever who is already convinced of the rightness of forgiveness, for example, and who notices that eschatological hope has the property of intensifying its rationality, will find in that property a reason to appropriate the hope. Maybe not a sufficient reason, but a reason nonetheless. Likewise, as I have argued elsewhere, unbelievers who believe in the equal dignity of all human beings, and who encounter the claims of a number of philosophers (some of them atheist) that such dignity has no secure home outside of a theological vision of things, are thereby given a reason to adopt that vision.[5] So, in addition to making an ethical case that is authentic, Christians also have an apologetic motive for making clear its relevant theological elements. And I can see no good reason why challenging one's interlocutors to think again about their fundamental view of things should not be part of public discourse. Parliamentary debates and the jurisprudential explanations of judges may not be proper sites for a full and frank exchange about such ultimate matters, but they can surely accommodate skirmishes.

Part of what determines whether a religious argument is behaving properly in public is the relevance of its content to its context. What is appropriate in an ecclesial public will not necessarily be appropriate in

5. Nigel Biggar, *Aiming to Kill: The Ethics of Suicide and Euthanasia* (London: Darton, Longman and Todd, 2004), pp. xii-xiii, 180n.87; Biggar, "Not Translation, but Conversation: Theology in Public Debate about Euthanasia," in *Religious Voices in Public Places,* ed. Nigel Biggar and Linda Hogan (Oxford: Oxford University Press, 2009), p. 159n.3.

a secular one. A sheer appeal to authority might be appropriate in the first, but not in the second. Nevertheless, in a secular public, biblical references might embellish a moral argument without losing its audience. Furthermore, moral arguments that depend on theological elements should not be shy of stating them, for unbelievers who gag at swallowing them whole might still manage part; and once they recognize the good ethical service that the theological element performs, they will find the latter at least meaningful — perhaps also palatable.

Content, however, is not all. The other part of what makes a theological argument behave in public is its manner. Certainly, the selection of content itself signifies respect or disrespect; but so does the manner of its delivery and, more broadly, the manner in which conversation as a whole is conducted. Christians bear witness to what they believe at least as much in how they speak as in what they say. If they believe in human creatureliness and sinfulness and in the eschatological futurity of perfect understanding, and if they believe in these seriously — that is, as applying *to themselves* — then Christians will come to public discussion with the virtue of docility. They will come ready to listen, perhaps to learn, maybe even to change their mind.

By the same token, they will come with a certain virtue of tolerance, ready to entertain disagreeable points of view and to consider them. This need not, and should not, be the degenerate liberal version, which does not care what others think so long as they do not get in the way. Instead of this tolerance-as-indifference, the Christian will display a readiness to engage with the other and his alien views in common subjection to the one (if not simple) truth about the coherent world of the only God's creating. The Christian virtue of tolerance will issue, not out of cynicism and carelessness, but out of love — for the truth and for the human well-being that depends on it. Furthermore, Christian tolerance will not be lazily infinite: it will be aware that not everything should be entertained, that some things must be resolutely gainsaid. Nevertheless, it will be cautious in deciding where to draw the line, acutely conscious that its very own Lord himself suffered death at the hands of those who judged him intolerably heterodox.

In addition to docility and tolerance-as-care, the Christian will bring to public deliberation the virtue of charity. This may involve more

71

than respect, but it will not involve less. The Christian will regard the other as a fellow creature who also stands in relationship to God, but whose relationship is immediate, inimitable, and different from her own. She will recognize that the other's vocation is uniquely the other's. She will cede the other space, acknowledging his difference. She will approach him as a potential prophet, as one who might yet mediate a true word of God. In this theological sense, therefore, she will respect the other as equal — and yet not the same. She will not assume that he has nothing worth saying. She will not presume to know what the other thinks before she has first bothered to inquire and listen. She will not stereotype or caricature him. She will not assimilate him to some ideal type, for example, "liberal" or "modernist" or "conservative" or "fundamentalist." Instead, she will listen to his particular, complex, idiosyncratic, and unpredictable views, which refuse easy accommodation in any prefabricated box. She will respect the other by taking him as he actually comes.

However, there is indeed more to charity than respect. For the sake of giving to the truth maximal space for an epiphany, the Christian will construe the other's point of view in the strongest, not the weakest, terms. She will forswear straw men. After all, her aim is to learn, not to dominate. So if the other has something to teach, not to learn it is to fail. The Christian, then, will be generous in giving credit where credit is due.

On the other hand, charity is not the same as deference, and the Christian will not shy away from contradicting. The virtue of charity should make room for the virtue of critical candor. After all, if the point of public conversation is to approximate the truth about public goods more nearly, then the Christian has a responsibility to contribute her perception of things, and that involves denying what she thinks should be denied. But the manner of her denial will be fraternal. "No!" will be uttered as one creature and sinner to another, not as the righteous to the unrighteous. This will mean that it is never uttered in a patronizing tone; for, again, the point of conversation is to persuade or change, not to humiliate or domineer.

Having said that, the example of Jesus himself prevents us from saying that the Christian should never contradict strongly, even angrily and fiercely. In Matthew 23:13-33, Jesus rails against his antagonists: "But woe to you, scribes and Pharisees, hypocrites!" (seven times); denounces them as "blind guides" (twice), "blind fools" (twice), "blind Pharisee" (once); and ends by thundering, "You serpents, you brood of vipers! How are you to escape being sentenced to hell?" (Matt. 23:33). The tone here is hardly measured and urbane. Conversation and persuasion have given way to outright condemnation, as sometimes it must, when the problem is not ignorance but stubborn injustice. The terms of condemnation are very fierce. Are they intemperate or abusive or violent? Arguably not, insofar as they are proportionate to the vice they contradict. So much vice deserves so much hostility. Angry denunciation is the last resort of contradiction, when all other means — all means of dialectical persuasion — have run themselves into the sand. As, indeed, they sometimes do.

So the Christian contribution to public discourse cannot confine itself to the modes of sweet reason. The prophetic strands in the biblical narrative, including the New Testament, forbid it. This is, of course, very dangerous talk, because angry denunciation does tend to provoke physical violence — as it did in Jesus' case. To legitimate denunciation at all, even only as a last resort, is to give a hostage to the fortunes of impatience. But Christians have no choice here, I think. Sometimes wickedness is very, very stubborn. Sometimes it will not be moved by persuasion, and it cannot be met with silence. Sometimes, then, the Christian must stop being wise man and start playing prophet.

If that is so, then patience is not an absolute virtue: it does not apply always and everywhere. Sometimes it should cease, as it did in Jesus' conduct toward the scribes and Pharisees. Sometimes peace is so willfully distorted that we must risk its disruption. However, if impatience is sometimes a virtue, most of the time it remains a vice. It becomes a virtue when grave vice is evidently shameless and resolute, and when continuing patience would be a form of evasion or complicity. Before that point, however, Christian conversation should be patient, even in the face of views that seem highly suspect. Initial engagement between strangers is often defensive and brittle. Trust takes time to develop, and fruitful exchange — involving candor and concession — can only take place in a climate of trust.

Sometimes communication may seem pointless, like trying to argue with a drunk. Sometimes one's interlocutor may be relentlessly dogmatic, refusing to give a moment's serious consideration to alternative viewpoints. Further conversation may have every appearance of being a complete waste of breath, and an impatient breaking off may seem like an eminently sensible thing to do. And yet, committed ideologues have been known to change their minds, be they members of the I.R.A., for example, or militant Islamists.[6] The causes of conversion are various. The most immediate will include a growing — and eventually intolerable — awareness of internal discrepancies and inconsistencies. This awareness may be born of direct, unmediated perception.[7] But it may also be sparked or enhanced by observations made, and questions posed, in the course of an exchange with patient outsiders. Attempts at reasonable conversation with ideologues may appear futile. But short-term appearances can deceive: subversive fruit takes time to grow.

Sometimes, however, patience will have to amount to more than just resilience and persistence. Sometimes it will have to become those parts of charity that are forbearance and forgiveness. Actual conversations, especially over matters of passionate concern, are often discol-

6. Here I am thinking of Séan O'Callaghan, who turned informer against the Irish Republican Army, and Eamonn Collins, who left it; and of Ed Husain, Hassan Butt, Shiraz Maher, and Maajid Nawaz, who abandoned British militant Islamism.

7. O'Callaghan and Collins became disillusioned with the I.R.A. through their experience of things that simply did not square with Irish Republican ideology. In O'Callaghan's case, it was the presence of grotesque sectarian animosity among his I.R.A. comrades (*The Informer* [London: BCA, 1998], pp. 82-83); in Collins's case, it was the experience of scrupulous justice at the hands of a British judge (*Killing Rage* [London: Granta, 1997], pp. 339-41). Likewise, Husain abandoned militant Islamism in part because of its lack of spiritual, moral, and theological integrity (*The Islamist* [London: Penguin, 2007], pp. 101, 114, 128, 174-75, 188, 222, 231, 241, 244-45, 256, 282); Butt, it seems, because of the disjunction between the present situation of British-born Muslims and the context assumed by traditional Islamic theology (Hassan Butt, "My Plea to Fellow Muslims: You Must Renounce Terror," *The Observer,* July 1, 2007); and Maher and Nawaz, because of exposure to the historically plural nature of Islamic tradition, which is at odds with the monolithic story of Islam sold them by Hizb ut-Tahrir (Shiraz Maher, "How I Escaped Islamism," *The Sunday Times,* August 12, 2007, p. 19; Maajid Nawaz, "Why I Joined the British Jihad — and Why I Rejected It," *The Sunday Times,* September 16, 2007, News Review, p. 8).

ored by acts of disrespect, unfairness, humiliation, deliberate provocation, evasive sleights of hand, willful distortion, or vicious impatience. In the face of such communicative vices and injuries, then, the Christian will follow his Lord in exercising the virtues of forbearance and forgiveness, for the sake of the truth and the human well-being that depends on it. He will be aware of his own creaturely fatedness and his own sinfulness; and he will be kept hopeful by the prospect of the Apocalypse, when all that is hidden will be brought to light. And since the Christian, sinner that he still is, has probably inflicted injury as well as suffered it, he must exercise the virtue of repentance in asking for forgiveness, as well as the virtue of compassion in granting it.

Docility, tolerance-as-care, charity-as-respect and charity-as-optimal-construal, critical candor (even in the ultimate form of denunciation), impatience with grave and shameless vice, patience with anything less, charity in granting forgiveness, and repentance in asking for it — these are among the virtues that should govern the manner of Christians' conversation and should cause them to *behave* in public.

But perhaps these virtues, and the moral ideal of conversation that they comprise, are too elitist, too academic. Academics may be trained to be scrupulously careful and circumspect in their engagement with alien points of view, but other people are not. Can one really expect public figures, for example, to engage with opponents openly, respectfully, patiently, and charitably? The first thing to say is that it would be nice to think that academics *were* all trained in these communicative virtues. They should be, but they are not. As universities have grown embarrassed about their medieval Christian heritage, and shy of assuming any spiritually or morally formative roles, they have come to train academics to be clever rather than wise, to win rather than learn, to dominate rather than contribute. Logical, analytical, literary, and rhetorical skills do not add up to good reasoning. Such technical expertise cannot protect reasoning from being driven and distorted by pride, contempt, cruelty, lust, vicious impatience, and fear. Second, while honest communication and good reasoning seem rare in public discussion, they are not entirely absent. Indeed, it has been said of Barack Obama that he is so persuasive in debate because, before he sets out to criticize his opponent's position, he first takes care to restate it accurately.[8] Such a practice may well be rhetorically and politically prudent; but it is also an expression of charity. Third, the apparent rarity of virtuous communication and reasoning may well be caused by cynical attitudes and adversarial practices of the media, rather than rooted in the essence of political life.[9] And fourth, however rare virtue may be in public discourse, public life cannot afford its absence. After all, public decisions that are arrogant, unteachable, uncharitable, impatient, and careless with the truth will be bad, distorted, unwise decisions, which do real damage to institutions and individuals.

So communicative virtue is not the preserve of an academic elite. Nor is it a luxury that public life can do without. This then raises the question of its social matrix, of where in a society one might hope to find it generated, and that brings us back to the churches. Given what Christians say they believe — about the basic rationality of things, about the equal dignity of human creatures, about the limits of their cognitive and moral powers, about human solidarity in sin, about the divinely confirmed norm of forgiveness, about eschatological hope for the apocalypse, and about patience in the meantime — one should expect the churches to form their members in corresponding virtues that qualify their manner of communication. Given the Christian creed, one should expect Christian churches to be nurseries of communicative virtues of the kind that I have described.

For this reason, the way churches conduct their own internal controversies is a vital test of their own integrity, a vital part of their witness to the rest of the world, and a vital part of their contribution to its well-being. So, for example, how the Anglican Communion handles its cur-

8. In this practice, it seems that Obama stands in a tradition going back through Benjamin Cardozo to John Stuart Mill: "He [Cardozo] never disguised the difficulties, as lazy judges do who win the game by sweeping all the chessmen off the table: like John Stuart Mill, he would often begin by stating the other side better than its advocate had stated it himself" (Learned Hand, "Mr. Justice Cardozo," *Harvard Law Review* 52 [1939]: 362).

9. In *What the Media are Doing to Our Politics* (London: Constable and Robinson, 2004), John Lloyd, an editor of *The Financial Times,* argues that the British media tend to operate in terms of a self-flattering, cynical master-narrative about politicians, which naturally puts the latter on the defensive and closes down open public discussion. See, e.g., the introduction to his book.

rent strife over the ordination of homosexuals to the priesthood and of women to the episcopate is of far more than merely local interest. Rather than a huge and tragic distraction from the church's mission (as I used to think them), these persistent quarrels are actually a major opportunity for the Christian churches to become what they should be, to embody what they believe, to bear theological witness in the manner of their being, and to offer a salutary and hopeful example to the rest of the world. After all, where is the public whose discourse is not distorted by pride and fear, by caricature and resentment? And where is the public that rejoices in a natural surplus of careful tolerance and proportionate candor, of patience and forgiveness? If, to use some of Rowan Williams's words, Anglicans can accept the secular imperfection of their church, eschewing fantasies of ecclesial purity, admitting that the other is here to stay, and deciding to live with the fact of persistent disagreement; if they can acknowledge that this disagreement is not merely the result of *someone else's* unfaithfulness or prejudice; and if they can keep their tolerance engaged with love for the truth, rather than letting it grow indifferent with carelessness — then maybe they will succeed in finding "the forms of agreed self-restraint that will allow [them] to keep conversation alive."[10] And if they do succeed, then they will have learned how to make theological arguments behave in public. And having learned, they may teach.

So, can a theological argument behave in public? Yes, it can. But the

---

10. Rowan Williams, "Archbishop's Presidential Address," delivered to the General Synod of the Church of England on February 10, 2009: www.bishopofcanterbury.org/ 2169: "[T]he Lambeth conference [of 2008] established . . . a climate in which every participant is guaranteed a hearing . . . the difficult but unavoidable search for the forms of agreed self-restraint that will allow us to keep conversation alive. . . . The Communion we have: it is indeed a very imperfect thing. . . . [W]e have to recognize that the other person or community or tradition is not simply going to go *away*. . . . All of us — and I do emphatically mean liberals as well as traditionalists — have a bit of us that is in love with purity, that wants to find in the other a perfect echo of ourselves and to be able to present to the world outside a united face, whether of clear commitments to the liberties and dignities of humanity as seen in the modern world or unswerving fidelity to the faith delivered to the saints — or both, of course. . . . Anglicanism has always . . . [had] a keen pragmatic awareness of the oddity and resilience of flesh and blood, the diversity of personal perception or reception of the common heritage. . . . [S]ome dreams of purity and clarity are not going to be realized."

notion of "behaving" connotes a naughty child forced to conform resentfully to a parent's alien rule. It connotes heteronomy. Here, however, the rules that govern the content and manner of theological argument are autonomous, in the sense that they come from within a Christian theological vision of things, not from outside it. For sure, these may well overlap with norms generated by other visions; after all, Christians are hardly the only ones who value respect and tolerance. But what exactly it is that they respect, and how exactly they are tolerant, will be relatively distinctive, as will the importance that they ascribe to the exercise of forgiveness. So, yes, a theological argument can — and should — behave in public, but on its own grounds and sometimes in its own way.

CHAPTER 5

So, What Is the Church Good For?

My argument about how Christians should behave in the public deliberation of a polyglot society has depended crucially on a certain view of the church and its relationship to the wider world. That has come to the surface, but only intermittently and often obliquely. Now it is time for me to put my ecclesiological cards on the table.

One of the most salient developments in recent Christian theology generally, and in recent Christian ethics in particular, has been renewed reflection on the church. To some extent this ecclesiological turn is a healthy sign of renewed self-confidence among Christians, a confidence that Christianity has something worthwhile to say. It has to be good that Christians do not feel so much the need to hide their identity, lest they be thought primitive and irrational by soi-disant moderns. It has to be good that apologists of the faith do not take its cultured despisers so seriously as to feel it necessary to camouflage the particularity of Christianity and talk about it only obliquely, and at a respectable, "scientific" distance, in terms of (supposedly) universal "religion."[1] To talk of the church is to talk openly of a particular, historical society with a particular tradition of thought; it is to assume that that tradition of thought has something to say that is worth listening to.

---

1. I think here of Reinhold Niebuhr in *Moral Man and Immoral Society* (1931). What is true of Niebuhr in that book, however, is not true of him in *An Interpretation of Christian Ethics* (1935) or in *The Nature and Destiny of Man* (1941; 1943).

79

Contemporary talk of the church, however, is also about a particular tradition of practice. There is a salutary recognition abroad today that the church does not speak only in its sermons, episcopal statements, papal encyclicals, working party reports, and theological tomes. It also speaks in the manner of its being. It speaks in its liturgical rites, in its institutional structures and procedures, and in the behavior of its members. Indeed, it is surely in its practice that the church speaks most effectively, since most human beings have a limited tolerance for elaborate words and arguments and are moved first and foremost by the beauty of the truth that they see embodied in the goodness of flesh-and-blood human beings, which commands their admiring attention. Therefore, talk about the church these days is quite properly talk about the particular social ethos that the particular Christian view of the world generates, and that forms the self-understanding and ruling dispositions of its members. The Christian church *shows* its vision of things quite as much as it *states* it.

The recent turn of Christian ethics to ecclesiology, then, is bound up with its turn to the formation of virtue. Moral life is not primarily about analysis, deliberation, or reflection. If it were, it would be the preserve of an articulate, educated elite. On the contrary, moral life is primarily about the ordering of attitudes and dispositions, curbing some and growing others. Most fundamentally, it is about the education of desire or love.

Here morality merges with spirituality. "Spirituality," of course, is a vague term that is now put to all kinds of use, some of them testing the bounds of coherence. In Christian hands, however, it refers to the human being's relationship with God. To use Karl Barth's terms, it has to do with the "vertical" rather than the "horizontal." As a human being understands God, so he understands himself; and as he understands himself, so he disposes himself with respect to those around him. If, as Trinitarian Christians believe, God is Creator, Forgiver, and ultimate Redeemer, then human beings, correlatively, are sinful creatures, already recipients of God's embracing compassion, yet still awaiting the completion of redemption. This self-understanding generates dispositions toward God of humility (born both of creaturely dependence and of sinfulness), gratitude (both for creaturely being and for forgiveness), and hope. These theological or spiritual or vertical dispositions then generate horizontal ones toward fellow human beings, such as a lack of self-righteousness, docility (that is, a readiness to learn from others), compassion for those who do one wrong, and patience in the face of persistent prejudice.

These dispositions are not universally regarded as virtues. For example, the very fact that I felt the need to specify "docility" in that last sentence indicates that, in modern culture, to be "docile" is to be childish, slavish, sheeplike. Modern, grown-up, autonomous people think for themselves; they do not need others to tell them what to do. Similarly, contemporary disciples of Nietzsche (and maybe of Aristotle, too) are unlikely to think well of people who respond with patience and compassion to those who do them wrong. That the absence of self-righteousness and the presence of docility, compassion, and patience are seen as virtues, not vices, is determined by their location in a Christian theological narrative vision of the world. In this vision their status as virtues makes sense: in this vision they are morally *rational*. And it is this particular vision that is preserved in the church and handed down over the generations through it: in its reading of Scripture, its creeds, and its sacramental rites.

I have no quarrel with the ecclesiological turn of recent Christian ethics — as such. On the contrary, it seems to me entirely salutary in principle. In practice, however, there are problems. To affirm the church and Christian identity, to tell the truth as Christians see it, and to criticize opposing views is one thing; but to caricature and denigrate the world is quite another. Indeed, there are serious theological problems with talking in terms of "Church" and "World" at all. It is true that this language of stark opposition is present in the New Testament, most consistently in the Johannine literature. I do not doubt that there are times and places in history where Christian churches have found — or will find — themselves in an environment that is viciously hostile and grossly unjust. In such situations it is understandable that Christians should come to see their environment as the epitome of evil and so to talk of the world as "the World." Understandable, yes, but dangerous. Such a dualistic tendency should be given pause by Jesus' own extraordinary behavior on the cross: "Father, forgive them," Luke has him say of his executioners, "for they know not what they do" (Luke 23:34). Here the Father of Light steps across the divide and stands for a moment in the shoes of the Children of Darkness. Would that the children of Light always followed suit. Would that they were always the children of *this* light, so courageous and generous in its sympathy.

Jesus seriously muddied the waters between the Church and the World. Taking up a major complaint of the classical Hebrew prophets, he warned the self-styled "people of God" not to presume upon their status. Ignoring the proprietary assumptions of the would-be gatekeepers of God's kingdom, he set about growing it in social circles that flouted their criteria. Saint Paul's pushing open the heavy gates of Judaism to let in Gentiles of "faith" was a direct extension of Jesus' liberalizing impulse. One of the most salient morals of the tale of the origins of Christianity is that the Spirit of God blows where it wills, and that even the pious — with all their prayers and all their theologizing — are really rather poor at predicting its whereabouts. Actually, the moral is even sharper: that the pious, confusing their piety with property, not only fail to track God's presence but actually obstruct it. That is surely part of the meaning of the cross, since the Gospels present the high priests and "the people," rather than the Romans, as the prime movers in engineering Jesus' death.

The ecclesiological implication of this is that the true "people of God" comprises those who are open to discovering God's kingdom in unlikely and unpromising quarters. The true church is not entirely confident of its own faithfulness and not quite certain of its own boundaries. Accordingly, it approaches apparent infidels, not naively or uncritically, but with a certain curiosity, wondering whether God's Spirit might be operating even among them. Ironically, then, the true church manifests itself precisely among those who cannot quite see the world as "the World" because they cannot quite see themselves as "the Church."

Karl Barth captures this subtle position better than most. On the one hand, Barth leaves no one in doubt that the church's historic witness to the Incarnation of God in Jesus Christ, and its tradition of reflection on the human situation in its light, is something that the world needs to hear. Nor can one doubt that Barth affirms the role of the church in the moral formation of Christians; after all, the very core of his mature theological ethics is the Lord's Prayer, flanked by the rites of baptism and the Lord's Supper.[2] Nor can one doubt that ethical deliberation has, in his view, an essential ecclesial dimension.[3] Barth's decision to change the title of his magnum opus from "Christian Dogmatics" to "Church Dogmatics" was no act of whimsy.

On the other hand, as I have already indicated in chapter 1, Barth's ecclesiology ends up being generously extrovert.[4] It seems to me quite true to say of him, as did Hans Urs von Balthasar, that he is "as open to the world and takes as much joy in it as any theologian around."[5] Notwithstanding his unambiguous affirmation of the importance of the church's speaking, Barth insisted on the importance of the church's also listening, and not just primarily to the Word of God in Scripture, but also secondarily to the Word of God in the world. "In the narrow corner in which we have our place and task," he says, "we cannot but eavesdrop in the world at large."[6] One basic theological reason for this lies in the precarious contingency of the reality of the church upon the forgiving grace of God. The real church exists only where and when its members dispose themselves toward God in humility and repentance:

> The real Church therefore lives as if constantly held and sustained over an abyss. When it imagines it can find comfort and encouragement in itself it is certainly not the real Church. The real Church lives on the comfort and exhortation which it is allowed to receive despite the folly and perversity of man. . . . It lives by allowing itself to be shamed by His [its Lord's] goodness. It

2. See Nigel Biggar, *The Hastening That Waits: Karl Barth's Ethics*, rev. ed. (Oxford: Clarendon Press, 1993), pp. 67-81, 127-45.

3. Biggar, *The Hastening That Waits*, pp. 123-26.

4. What follows on this and on the next three pages is largely a précis of pp. 147-51 of *The Hastening That Waits*.

5. Hans Urs von Balthasar, *The Theology of Karl Barth*, trans. Edward T. Oakes, SJ (San Francisco: Ignatius Press, 1992), p. 197.

6. Karl Barth, *Church Dogmatics*, vol. IV, *The Doctrine of Reconciliation*, trans. G. W. Bromiley (Edinburgh: T. & T. Clark, 1961), pt. 3.1, p. 117.

lives only in so far as its own religiosity and pious habits, its whole ritual . . . are constantly being reduced to dust and ashes in the fire of His Word and Spirit.[7]

The members of this real church, therefore, are "neither religious virtuosi nor a moral elite," but "lost sinners" who "are more aware of the extent of human guilt before God, are more aware than others of the indissoluble solidarity of all men as sinners."[8] Because of this self-awareness, they are bound to relate to those (who seem to be) outside of the church in "moral fellowship" and with a disposition of openness.

This openness, however, is grounded not simply in an awareness of common sinfulness but also in the truly social nature of human being. Real human being, Barth tells us, is being in encounter, which involves a reciprocal and benevolent looking in the eye and a reciprocal speaking and hearing, by which he means that the self and the other enter into a common life, where "they continually have to take each other into practical account."[9] To participate in this real, redeemed, fulfilled humanity is to be free from the sin of pride, which inclines the creature to pretend to godlike moral wisdom and to surrender himself to the ideological thinking and strife "in which at bottom no one understands the language of others because he is much too convinced of the soundness of his own seriously to want to understand the others."[10]

Whence does Barth get this vision of real, or fulfilled, humanity? He claims to have found it revealed in Christ — or, more exactly, in Jesus as the God-man — who, on the one hand, draws alongside human beings as their fellow, and on the other hand, responds to God's initiative by becoming his covenant-*partner*.[11] To this high christological source he

7. Karl Barth, "The Real Church," in *Against the Stream,* ed. R. G. Smith, trans. E. M. Delacour and Stanley Godman (London: SCM, 1954), pp. 67-68.

8. Barth, "The Real Church," p. 67.

9. Karl Barth, *Church Dogmatics,* vol. III, *The Doctrine of Creation,* trans. Harold Knight et al., pt. 2 (Edinburgh: T. & T. Clark, 1960), p. 253.

10. Karl Barth, *Church Dogmatics,* vol. IV, *The Doctrine of Reconciliation,* trans. G. W. Bromiley, pt. 1 (Edinburgh: T. & T. Clark, 1956), p. 447.

11. See Barth, *Church Dogmatics,* III/2, S.45.2, "The Basic Form of Humanity," pp. 222-84.

could have added corroboration from the text of the New Testament, with its recurrent theme of the reciprocal exchange of status — of the last becoming first, lords becoming servants, and rabbis washing disciples' feet. Most of all, he could have referred to the famous passage in the Revelation of John, where God in Christ not merely promises "that if any one hears my voice and opens the door, I will come in to him and eat with him," but add — marvelously surrendering the benefactor's initiative — "and he with me" (Rev. 3:20).[12]

There is yet a third theological ground for the virtue of openness: the secular phenomenon of "potential" Christians. Echoing one of Jesus' mantras, Barth tells us that "there are no last who might not be found among the first."[13] In the case of both confessing Christians and confessing non-Christians, their destiny lies in front of them. As the former have not yet arrived, so the latter might yet set out:

12. While the general contours of an anthropology in which reciprocity is central might have first impressed themselves on Barth as he contemplated the higher reaches of Christology, it is difficult to resist the thought that the particular terms in which he elaborated on the theme of reciprocity ("I," "Thou," "It," "encounter") were borrowed — or better, annexed — from the "philosophy of dialogue" that flourished in the 1920s and 1930s and had its precursors in Hermann Cohen's Neo-Kantianism, Feuerbach, and Kierkegaard (Dieter Becker, *Karl Barth und Martin Buber — Denker in dialogischer Nachbarschaft? Zur Bedeutung Martin Bubers für die Anthropologie Karl Barths* [Göttingen: Vanderhoeck und Rupprecht, 1986], pp. 39, 43-47). While Barth does not admit any particular debt to Martin Buber, he does acknowledge points of overlap between his own Christian anthropology and Buber's Jewish one; and the terms in which he acknowledges them are relevant to our discussion of Christian regard for non-Christians: "In this respect theological anthropology has to go its own way, and as it pursues it resolutely to the end it is led to statements which are very similar to those in which humanity is described from a very different angle (e.g., by . . . the Jew M. Buber). But does this constitute any good reason why we should not make them? Of course, if we look carefully, there can be no question of an exact correspondence and coincidence between the Christian statements and these others which rest on very different foundations. We need not be surprised that there are approximations and similarities. . . . And surely it need not be, and is not actually, the case, that . . . worldly wisdom with its very different criteria has always been mistaken. . . . Even with his natural knowledge of himself the natural man is still in the sphere of divine grace . . ." (*Church Dogmatics*, III/2, p. 277). In fact, Dieter Becker has discovered evidence that Barth not only overlapped with Buber but was somewhat influenced by him (Becker, *Karl Barth und Martin Buber*, pp. 191-216).

13. Karl Barth, *Church Dogmatics*, vol. III, *The Doctrine of Creation*, trans. A. T. Mackay et al., pt. 4 (Edinburgh: T. & T. Clark, 1961), p. 484.

[A]s Christians and therefore as those who are called we are constrained to be absolutely open in respect of all other men without exception, exercising towards them the same openness as that in which alone, because the event of our calling can never be behind us in such a way that it is not also before us, we can see and understand ourselves as those who are called. . . . No man who is called does not also have to see and understand himself as one who still has to be called and therefore as one who stands alongside and in solidarity with the uncalled. . . . For all the seriousness with which we must distinguish between Christians and non-Christians, we can never think in terms of rigid separation. All that is possible is a genuinely unlimited openness of the called in relation to the uncalled, and unlimited readiness to see in the aliens of today the brothers of tomorrow.[14]

This is not to say that Christians should try to pass the non-Christian off as "really a Christian . . . in view of the certain higher aspects of his character," for that would be the death of Christian responsibility with respect to him. Nevertheless,

the fact remains that in the existence of these others there is something that has to be taken more seriously, and indeed infinitely more seriously from the qualitative standpoint, than their blatant non-Christianity in one form or another, namely the fact that, no matter who or what they are or how they live, their vocation is before them no less surely than that Jesus Christ has died and risen again for them. . . . It is the one sure thing we know concerning them. Anything we know concerning the fact that they are not called and not Christians can finally be only a matter of more or less well-founded conjecture. And even where we think we can be most sure of the fact, the reference can only be to what they are or are not provisionally.[15]

14. Karl Barth, *Church Dogmatics,* vol. IV, *The Doctrine of Reconciliation,* trans. G. W. Bromiley, pt. 3.2 (Edinburgh: T. & T. Clark, 1961), p. 493.
15. Barth, *Church Dogmatics,* IV/3.2, p. 493.

Therefore, on these three theological grounds — common sinful-ness and dependence on God's forgiving grace, the reciprocal nature of real human being, and uncertainty about others' final destiny — Barth urges that the Christian should be open to hearing God's Word from the lips of the apparently indifferent and godless, for "it may be that the Lord has bidden those outside the Church to say something important to the Church. The Church therefore has every reason not to ignore the questions and warnings of the outside world."[16]

When I first encountered this view of Barth more than fifteen years ago, I found it compelling. I find it even more compelling now. Why? Partly because a Christian theological anthropology does seem to imply it; but also because my experience has confirmed it. Individuals are sel-dom, if ever, simply representatives of a fixed, discrete worldview, be it theological or philosophical. Indeed, a worldview itself is neither fixed nor discrete. Rather it is constantly developing in relationship to other worldviews, sometimes defining itself over and against them, some-times adopting and modifying some of their features. Further, a worldview is seldom, if ever, a single system, but rather a collection of species that share a common historical origin and some common be-liefs and practices, but that differ from each other in their interpreta-tions of the common heritage in the ways they arrange the common ele-ments and the relative weight that they ascribe to each of them.

Further still, not all of the adherents of a species of a particular worldview can be presumed to believe and practice exactly the same things in exactly the same way. There is often a considerable discrep-ancy between the classic or official stance of a worldview and the stances taken by its members. For example, there are many members of orthodox Christian churches who weekly recite one of the classic creeds, but neither understand the doctrine of the Trinity nor have it play any significant part in their lives. Therefore, it is simply not enough to ask whether someone is a Christian or a Jew, a religious believer or an atheist, a conservative or a liberal. We need to know what kind of Chris-tian he is. But more than that, we need to know his particular construal

16. Barth, "The Christian Understanding of Revelation," in *Against the Stream*, pp. 228-29.

of whatever kind of Christianity he belongs to, which particular convictions and practices he holds dear and which he holds loosely, and why. Otherwise, we risk mistaking an individual for a specimen.

So, for example, if you want to understand where I stand in matters of belief and practice, you would need to know far more about me than the fact that I am a Christian. You would need to inquire, "What kind of Christian?" To which I would answer, "Anglican." "But what kind of Anglican?" you ask. "Well, one who is theologically orthodox and Protestant." "Ah!" you exclaim, "an evangelical!" Now you think that you have me. Generic labels, however, are not enough, for there are none that fit me (or you) perfectly. In the end you must deal with me as a particular person. And when you do, you will discover that, while I am Protestant with regard to ecclesiology and the Lord's Supper, I am wont to say that we are saved by grace through faith *and* works, and not by grace through faith alone; that I am much impressed by the rational methodical nature of Thomist ethics; and that I have a strong penchant for casuistry. You might also discover that my understanding of the authority of Scripture is more "liberal" than you would expect of an evangelical, since I am prepared to dissent from Saint Paul in his blanket condemnation (if that is what it is) of homosexual practice. On the other hand, you might find me predictably "conservative" in that I believe that "God" denotes a living reality of a quasi-personal kind and is not merely a projection of human ideals or wishes, and that Jesus rose bodily from the dead. Further, you might find me alarmingly "conservative" in thinking democracy seriously problematic and in supporting the (weak) establishment of Christian religion, or you might find me suspiciously "liberal" in that I rejoice in a (finitely) plural culture. Certainly you will discover that I do not hold all that I believe with equal enthusiasm, and that at certain points I live more or less comfortably with internal contradictions. In short, my worldview is a unique constellation of beliefs and practices, and in order to get a good grip on where I stand, you would have to deal with me *in particular* and at close quarters.

Therefore, to discover that A is a religious believer and B an atheist, or C is a "conservative" and D a "liberal," or E is a Christian and F a Jew is really not to have discovered very much at all. Indeed, if one were to rest with the generic labels, one would probably be seriously mistaken. The real waters are much muddier, maybe more disconcerting, but also more interesting. For if I were to make the effort to get to know E and F better, I might be surprised to find (as indeed I have) much greater affinity with a Jew who believes that God is able and inclined to involve himself directly in the concrete and personal particulars of history than with a Christian who believes that God only operates in the world via general, impersonal laws.

My own experience of encountering other people, not least non-Christians and non-believers — my own experience of trying to keep the conversation with them honest and careful, of having my own expectations about them surprised, and of having to crawl out from under their projections — has served to alert me to the ecclesiological implications of Jesus' ambiguous relationship with the "people of God," and to confirm the ecclesiology and the ethic of communication that Barth draws out of his theological anthropology, soteriology, and eschatology.

Such ecclesiological views, however, are not common sense in Christian ethics today. They are not shared, for example, by Stanley Hauerwas, who is arguably the dominant force in the Anglo-Saxon corner of the field. To be sure, there are times when Hauerwas has taken a Barthian position. For example, in *Truthfulness and Tragedy* (1977), he tells us that "the church can learn from society more just ways of forming life."[17] And in *The Peaceable Kingdom* (1983), he says that the church and the world are

> companions on a journey that makes it impossible for one to survive without the other, though each constantly seeks to do so. They are thus more often enemies than friends, an enmity tragically arising from the church's attempt to deny its calling and service to the world — dismissing the world as irredeemable, or transforming its own servant status into a triumphant subordination of the world. But God has in fact redeemed the world, even if the world refuses to acknowledge its redemption. That is

17. Stanley Hauerwas, *Truthfulness and Tragedy: Further Explorations in Christian Ethics* (Notre Dame, IN: University of Notre Dame Press, 1977), p. 42.

why as Christians we may . . . find that people who are not Christians manifest God's peace better than we ourselves. . . .[18]

More recently, in his Gifford Lectures, published as *With the Grain of the Universe* (2001), Hauerwas acknowledges, without demur, that "[a]ccording to Barth, the Christian knows that the will of God has been fulfilled outside of the church. To the shame of the church, in fact, the will of God has often been better fulfilled outside of the church than within it. . . ."[19]

However, in these same lectures Hauerwas takes issue with Barth's attempt to steer a middle course between "principial" nonconformity to the world and "principial" assimilation.[20] What Barth presents as (prudential) "freedom to take a few steps or even to go a good way along either path as need requires,"[21] Hauerwas receives as "instability," which is "as likely to lead to unfaithfulness as faithfulness." Hauerwas wants the Christian life tied down here, whereas "Barth fails to specify the material conditions that would sustain his middle way." Hauerwas traces this deficiency to Barth's "overly cautious" account of the role of the church in the economy of God's salvation. From this ecclesiological root springs a second, prophetic deficiency: "Because the church cannot trust in its calling to be God's witness, Barth seems far too willing to leave the world alone." In order to substantiate this second complaint, Hauerwas refers us to the

18. Stanley Hauerwas, *The Peaceable Kingdom: A Primer in Christian Ethics* (Notre Dame, IN: University of Notre Dame Press, 1983), p. 101. I owe my awareness of an earlier Barthian phase of Hauerwas's ecclesiology to Eric Gregory: "His [Hauerwas's] more recent work . . . backtracks from his earlier affirmation of a Barthian ecclesiology under the pressure of his desire to identify a reliable site for the social practices of embodied Christian virtue" (*Politics and the Order of Love: An Augustinian Ethic of Democratic Citizenship* [Chicago: University of Chicago Press, 2008], p. 133).

19. Stanley Hauerwas, *With the Grain of the Universe: The Church's Witness and Natural Theology* (Grand Rapids: Brazos, 2001), p. 201.

20. "Principial" is, as far as I know, an English neologism that Geoffrey Bromiley uses on at least four occasions in his translation of *The Christian Life: Church Dogmatics, IV/4, Lecture Fragments* (Grand Rapids: Eerdmans, 1981), pp. 197-200, to render the German word *prinzipiell*. In this context it seems to speak of something — whether nonconformity or assimilation — as having been adopted, not merely as *a* principle, but as *the* single, absolute principle.

21. Barth, *The Christian Life*, p. 201.

very first volume of the *Church Dogmatics* (1932) and to *The Holy Spirit and the Christian Life* (1929), where Barth says (as Hauerwas tells it) "that Christian faithfulness should not involve challenging false notions of science, morality, or art on theological grounds."[22]

Hauerwas is both right and wrong here, but more wrong than right. He is right that Barth's specification of the norms of Christian life — and thus of the criteria by which to judge alternatives — is often frustratingly underdeveloped, as I have argued elsewhere.[23] He is surely wrong, however, to claim that this results in Barth's simply leaving the world alone and failing to challenge it. Indeed, Barth concludes the very section ("Church, Theology, Science") from the *Church Dogmatics* (I/1) that Hauerwas cites by telling us, on the one hand, that

> [a]s a human concern for truth, [theology] recognizes its solidarity with other such concerns now grouped under the name of science. It protests against the idea of an ontological exaltation above them such as might easily be suggested by its emphatic and distinctive designation by older writers as *doctrina* or even *sapientia*. It remembers that it is only a science and therefore that it is secular even as it works in its own relatively special way and in the highest spheres.[24]

Thus the moment of humble assimilation. But note what immediately follows:

> In not just resigning the title to others, with all due respect to the classical tradition, [theology] makes a necessary protest against a general concept of science which is admittedly pagan. It cannot do any harm even to the most stalwart representatives of this concept, or indeed to the whole university, to be reminded by the presence of the theologian among them that the quasi-religious

22. Hauerwas, *With the Grain*, pp. 202-3.
23. Nigel Biggar, "Karl Barth's Ethics Revisited," in *Commanding Grace: Karl Barth's Theological Ethics*, ed. Daniel Migliore (Grand Rapids: Eerdmans, 2010), pp. 42-49.
24. Barth, *Church Dogmatics*, vol. I, *The Doctrine of the Word of God*, trans. G. W. Bromiley, pt. 1 (Edinburgh: T. & T. Clark, 1975), p. 11.

certainty of their interpretation of the term is not in fact undisputed, that the tradition which commences with the name of Aristotle is only one among others, and that the Christian Church certainly does not number Aristotle among its ancestors.

Finally, in grouping itself among the sciences for all the radical and indeed indissoluble difference in the understanding of the term, theology shows that it does not take the heathenism of their understanding seriously enough to separate itself under another name, but that it reckons them as part of the Church in spite of their refusal of the theological task and their adoption of a concept of science which is so intolerable to theology. It believes in the forgiveness of sins, and not the final reality of a heathen pantheon.[25]

If that is not a challenge to the secularist university, then I do not know what is. What is more, this moment of dissent, together with the earlier one of assimilation, actually provides a rather good specification of what Barth's prudent, circumspect, and discriminating middle course can amount to. A middle course need not be unstable; it can be balanced. And no, balance need not be a milksop. On the contrary, judging by this instance, it can pack quite a punch. In fact, it is precisely *because* it is balanced that the punch does not swing out wildly but drives straight home.

As for *The Holy Spirit and the Christian Life,* Barth nowhere says that Christians should not challenge false notions of morality and art. What he does say is that Christians should take care not to presume that they themselves or anything they do is Christian simply, since whatever is *iustus* is also *peccator,* and thus that whatever purports to be "Christian" morality, art, and culture is also, to some extent, not Christian. Barth's target here is "our victorious modern Christendom" — and by implication the triumphalist ecclesiology that it involves.[26] Notwithstanding this, he does not see his classically Protestant insistence on constant

25. Barth, *Church Dogmatics,* I/1, 11.
26. Karl Barth, *The Holy Spirit and the Christian Life: The Theological Basis of Ethics,* trans. R. Birch Hoyle (Louisville: Westminster John Knox, 1993), pp. 37-38.

Christian and ecclesial humility as hamstringing critical witness, a point he makes perfectly clear toward the end of *The Holy Spirit and the Christian Life:*

> The child [of God] looks beyond the present, also beyond the dialectical paradox of "always sinner and always righteous," to the coming kingdom of his father. . . . The child of God will speak out and be a missionary whether he will or no, and will not allow himself to be muzzled by any tactics of church and state maneuvering and manipulation, in the midst of where he lives. . . . Because this child of God speaks, he does not ask what his hearers like, nor what the result will be, nor as to the consequences. He speaks because he must speak.[27]

So where is the excessive caution that Hauerwas claims to find here? Where is the diffidence in one's calling to be God's witness? I don't see it.

Whatever Hauerwas's earlier views, he now seems to consider ecclesial humility to be an ethical liability. He claims to find Barth insufficiently "catholic" because he does not acknowledge that "the community called the church is constitutive of the gospel proclamation."[28] Quite what he means by this is obscure, since he admits (in a footnote) that Barth "says explicitly: 'The church [*sic*] is the historical form of the work of the Holy Spirit and therefore the historical form of the faith.'"[29] So what does Hauerwas find lacking? If it is not the affirmation, then it must be the qualification. While the church does embody the Holy Spirit, in Barth's view, it does so only insofar as it is aware of its own sinfulness and radical contingency upon the forgiving grace of God. Hauerwas appears to want to suppress the theological qualification in order to make an unequivocal ecclesiological affirmation. Thus he endorses Joseph Mangina's claim that an adequate account of the role of

27. Barth, *Holy Spirit and Christian Life,* pp. 66-67.
28. Hauerwas, *With the Grain,* p. 145.
29. Hauerwas, *With the Grain,* p. 145n.9, quoting Barth, *Church Dogmatics,* vol. II, *The Doctrine of God,* trans. G. W. Bromiley et al., pt. 1 (Edinburgh: T. & T. Clark, 1957), p. 160. (In fact, Hauerwas cites pt. 2 by mistake.)

the Spirit involves "the acceptance of the church itself as the binding medium in which faith takes place. The medium is, if not the message, the condition of the possibility of grasping the message in its truth."[30] I fear that the Pharisees of the Gospels and the Judaizers of the Pauline Epistles could not have stated their position better. "The binding medium" — whom does it bind? Those who would find faith, of course, but also the Spirit who would give it.[31]

Over twenty years ago I mentioned to Stanley Hauerwas that I noticed in him a suspect tendency to talk about the church where Barth would talk about God. Later, Hauerwas graciously conceded in print that my observation might have force.[32] It seems to me, I regret to say,

---

30. Hauerwas, *With the Grain,* p. 145.

31. Ironically, Hauerwas has subjected Reinhold Niebuhr to the same fire that he has directed at Barth. Several years before he made his critique of Barth's ecclesiology in his Gifford Lectures, Hauerwas had criticized Niebuhr in similar terms. According to Niebuhr, "each religion, or each version of a single faith, seeks to proclaim its highest insights while yet preserving an humble and contrite recognition that all actual expressions of religious faith are subject to historical contingency and relativity. . . . Profound religion must recognize the difference between divine majesty and human creatureliness" (*The Children of Light and the Children of Darkness* [London: Nisbet, 1945], pp. 93-94). This Hauerwas takes to be representative of Protestant liberalism, according to which all religions should think of themselves as "expressions of a more determinative human condition — that is, as a knowledge available to everyone" ("The Democratic Policing of Christianity," in *Dispatches from the Front: Theological Engagements with the Secular* [Durham: Duke University Press, 1994], p. 104). However, such a reading is not quite fair. Niebuhr does affirm that each religion proclaims *its own* insights, and he implies that these are distinct rivals to alternatives — since if there were no rivalry, there would presumably be no need for restraint by humility. Nothing that Niebuhr says here precludes the possibility that one religion's insights might be superior to another's. Hauerwas then accuses Niebuhr of being unrelenting in his criticism of "the Catholic theory of the church as divine institution," which "lends itself particularly to the temptation of confusing relative with eternal values" (Reinhold Niebuhr, *Essays in Applied Christianity,* ed. D. B. Robertson [New York: Living Age Books, 1959], p. 200); and he complains that Niebuhr would have Catholics become Protestants in order to be responsible democrats ("Democratic Policing," p. 216n.23). Hauerwas evinces no concern here about the ecclesial temptation to presumption. I think that he should, not least because Jesus did. It seems to me that ecclesial triumphalists, whoever they may be, need to adopt classical Protestant ecclesiological humility in order to be responsible Christians — not just responsible democrats.

32. Stanley Hauerwas, "The Truth about God: The Decalogue as Condition for Truthful Speech," in *Sanctify Them in the Truth: Holiness Exemplified* (Edinburgh: T. & T. Clark, 1998), pp. 37-38.

that it still does.[33] Hauerwas shies away from admitting the ambiguity, instability, and contingency (upon God) of Christian and ecclesial life, because he fears that this drains the church of confidence and definite, dissident substance. He sees the vagueness with which Barth characterizes the Christian life as the effect of his "unstable" ecclesiology. I agree that the vagueness is unsatisfactory, but I doubt this attribution. I attribute the lack of ethical specification, not to a spiritually humble ecclesiology, but to a mistaken suspicion of casuistry and its rational methodicality.[34] In fact, Barth combines ecclesial humility with prophetic forthrightness, and it seems to me that such a combination violates no logical or psychological necessity. It makes perfectly good sense to say that one can be humble, self-critical, penitent, and docile, and yet still be obedient and faithful and courageous enough to speak it exactly as it is given one to see it — come what may. A bold witness can still be open to listening, even to reconsidering; and a genuinely Christian witness will be.

Lack of humility vitiates love. The other side of a lack of ecclesial humility is a failure to pay careful attention to the world and a tendency to represent it — and misrepresent it — in terms of pejorative preconceptions. Accordingly, in the final chapter that follows his critical analysis of Barth, Hauerwas speaks of the world in characteristically broadbrush abstractions: "Constantinianism," "liberalism," "modernity," "democracy," and "technocracy."[35] I have complained elsewhere that his engagement with political "liberalism" in particular is ad hoc, underdeveloped, and undiscriminating.[36] Liberal political thought is not

33. I am not alone in making this judgment. Nicholas M. Healy, for example, observes in Hauerwas a "(relative) lack of attention to God's action in our midst"; he suggests that "the difference God makes to the church needs to be made clearer. It remains unclear what difference the Word and the Spirit's active presence might make to descriptions of the church's being and life that are couched in social-philosophical categories like 'virtue' and 'narrative'" ("Karl Barth's Ecclesiology Reconsidered," *Scottish Journal of Theology* 57, no. 3 [2004]: 295-96).

34. See Biggar, "Karl Barth's Ethics Revisited," p. 48; see also Biggar, *Hastening That Waits,* pp. 40-41, 44-45, 163.

35. Hauerwas, *With the Grain,* pp. 216, 221, 222.

36. Biggar, "Is Stanley Hauerwas Sectarian?" in *Faithfulness and Fortitude: In Conversation with the Theological Ethics of Stanley Hauerwas,* ed. Mark Thiessen Nation and Samuel Wells (Edinburgh: T. & T. Clark, 2000), pp. 152-60.

all of a single kind. Indeed, some of it is not merely compatible with Christian belief but actually required by it. Hauerwas does not actually deny this, but he does ignore it.[37] He continues to essentialize liberalism as he continues to essentialize the World. Thus, in his Gifford Lectures he objects that "Constantinianism" holds that the validity of the church or Jesus Christ or the New Testament "is to be judged by standards derived from the world."[38] To which I would respond — as Barth would, I imagine — "Never mind the provenance, pay attention to the data." Or, to echo Wittgenstein, "Don't assume, look! And then discriminate."[39] If love requires more, surely it requires no less.

This theologically pathological tendency to idealize the church and denigrate the world is not confined to Stanley Hauerwas. On the one hand, John Milbank's ecclesiology does tend to be healthier.[40] He assures us that he does not "imagine the Church as Utopia,"[41] and he admits that the church can "even become a hellish anti-Church."[42] In his book *Being Reconciled,* at the very opening of the chapter entitled "Ecclesiology," he says:

[F]or now we glimpse dimly . . . [the] perfection [of the ecclesial counter-polity] within a process of reconciliation that is but fragmentarily realized — like a fleeting passage of an aerial creature amongst the trees, which we are scarcely sure we have glimpsed at all. . . . Redemption remains a vague rumour. . . . The Church is the brotherhood and sisterhood of . . . those cease-

---

37. Stanley Hauerwas, "Where Would I Be Without Friends?" in Nation and Wells, *Faithfulness and Fortitude,* pp. 325-26.

38. Hauerwas, *With the Grain,* p. 221.

39. Ludwig Wittgenstein, *Philosophical Investigations,* trans. G. E. M. Anscombe (Oxford: Blackwell, 1972), section 66: "Don't think, but look"; Rush Rhees, ed., *Ludwig Wittgenstein: Personal Recollections* (Oxford: Blackwell, 1981), p. 171: "I'll teach you differences." I owe my knowledge of these sayings of Wittgenstein to Chris Insole.

40. My reading of Milbank in this paragraph owes much to Eric Gregory, *Politics and the Order of Love,* pp. 136-38.

41. John Milbank, "Enclaves, or Where is the Church?" *New Blackfriars* 73, no. 861 (June 1992): 341.

42. John Milbank, *Theology and Social Theory: Beyond Secular Reason* (Oxford: Blackwell, 1990), p. 433.

lessly questing . . . for the Church itself. The latter is not a given, but arrives endlessly, in passing.[43]

If it is hard to discern the church, then it is hard to tell the world from it: "The Church, like grace, is everywhere."[44] "[A]ll human society in some degree foreshadows *ecclesia* and in this way always mediates some supernatural grace."[45] Accordingly, Milbank suggests that "[contemporary liberation theology's] 'base communities' where the lines between Church and world, spiritual and secular are blurred . . . might just conceivably be the nearest thing to . . . [the] contemporary exemplification [of the 'political Augustinianism' that he espouses]."[46] And of postmodernity he says: "I want in general to suggest that we regard [it], like modernity, as a kind of distorted outcome of energies first unleashed by the Church itself. If that is the case, then our attitude is bound to be a complex one. Not outright refusal, nor outright acceptance."[47]

So far, so nuanced. Elsewhere in Milbank's thought, however, the lines between the Church and the World thicken and solidify. Robert Markus has observed that in *Theology and Social Theory,* Milbank tends to conflate the two distinct senses in which Augustine speaks of the *civitas terrena* ("earthly city"): the narrower, eschatological sense of "the community of the proud and selfish, those predestined to be damned"; and the wider, empirical sense of "the 'realm of the merely practical,'" "the mixed society on earth comprising both virtuous and wicked members," "any actual, empirical society."[48] As a consequence of this conflation, whereas "empirical groups, institutions, and societies are, for Augustine, always and necessarily composites of the two cities [the *civitas dei* and the *civitas terrena*], taken in their strict eschatological mean-

43. John Milbank, *Being Reconciled: Ontology and Pardon* (London: Routledge, 2003), p. 105.

44. Milbank, *Being Reconciled,* p. 138.

45. John Milbank, "The Gift of Ruling: Secularization and Political Authority," *New Blackfriars* 85, no. 996 (March 2004): 231.

46. Milbank, *Theology and Social Theory,* p. 408.

47. Milbank, *Being Reconciled,* p. 196.

48. Robert Markus, *Christianity and the Secular* (Notre Dame, IN: University of Notre Dame Press, 2006), pp. 46-47.

ing,"[49] Milbank reads him as saying that "pagan political communities were fundamentally sinful"[50] and that "[t]he realm of the practical, cut off from the ecclesial, is quite simply a realm of sin."[51]

It is true that Milbank is (mis)interpreting Augustine here, but his own thought appears to run along these putatively Augustinian lines when, for example, he draws a stark contrast between the Church and the World in claiming that "Christian morality is a thing so strange, that it must be declared immoral or amoral according to all other norms and codes of morality."[52] *Simply* immoral or amoral according to *all* other moralities? That claim is as implausible as it is grand. One may expect that the more distinctly the Christian option is made to shine, the more the alternatives are cast into darkness; and so it is. As I have complained of Hauerwas, so Eric Gregory complains of Milbank: he takes "one [secularist] version of the liberal story to be the whole story." And "[f]or all his . . . postmodern desire to undermine theoretical essentialism, a lot of abstraction does a lot of work in his narrative."[53]

Gregory also observes that what applies to Milbank applies to many of his associates: "authors associated with Radical Orthodoxy identify liberal democracy with lots of 'isms': totalitarianism, paganism, terrorism, materialism, fascism, absolutism, technologism, fetishism, and gnosticism."[54] This claim is substantiated by Christopher Insole in the case of William Cavanaugh, who, while rightly disposing of the whiggish history of the liberal state, proceeds to tell a countertale that finds "*the* hidden meaning of liberalism" in nationalism, state absolutism, and war. According to Insole, however, "there is no 'liberal state' — a single absolutizing entity — at all in Cavanaugh's sense." Moreover, having discredited the whiggish story of liberalism, Cavanaugh effectively introduces "a whiggish history of the church."[55]

49. Markus, *Christianity and the Secular*, p. 47.

50. Milbank, *Theology and Social Theory*, p. 390.

51. Milbank, *Theology and Social Theory*, p. 406.

52. John Milbank, "Can Morality be Christian?" in *The Word Made Strange: Theology, Language, Culture* (Oxford: Blackwell, 1997), p. 219.

53. Gregory, *Politics and the Order of Love*, p. 141.

54. Gregory, *Politics and the Order of Love*, pp. 134, 128.

55. Christopher Insole, "Discerning the Theopolitical: A Response to Cavanaugh's Reimagining of Political Space," *Political Theology* 7, no. 3 (2006): 324-25 (italics added),

One of the reasons for the unsatisfactorily abstract and unattractively moralistic quality of Radical Orthodox theologians' social criticism lies, I think, in their tendency to reach for social, cultural, or political theory when they want to mediate between theological premises and practical judgments. If, instead, they were to spend more time reflecting on concrete cases — whether presented in the press or in history books or in pastoral experience — then their critical concepts would have to wrestle with awkward particulars and, should they survive, become less self-righteous and more discriminating, accurate, patient, and fair.[56]

To criticize fellow humans who are not confessing Christians, to challenge them with discriminating prophecy, belongs to Christian responsibility. But to stereotype and caricature and denigrate others — whether Christian or not — is to forget one's own status as *peccator* made *iustus* by God's grace, to fail in compassionate love for fellow sinners, and thereby to betray the gospel. There are, of course, plenty of other forms of betrayal, but this is surely one of them. We genuinely belong to Jesus' version of God's kingdom precisely insofar as we do *not* presume to know quite where the Spirit blows, and insofar as we are

---

329. My own ecclesiology resonates closely with Insole's: "The closest disciples of Jesus use their freedom to deny Jesus . . . betray him . . . and to flee and desert him. . . . Let us take seriously that *this* is the church, the early church, and reckon with what it means to be no better than the chosen and closest disciples (if there is to be no Whiggery, then let there be none). Throughout [the New Testament] we find the expected boundaries of who is 'inside' or who 'outside' subverted. Those who *do* show faith, understanding or a desire to follow Jesus are frequently strangers and outcasts. . . . We are called to . . . self-interrogation and humility not so much because of the 'not yet,' but because of the reversal in our expectations brought about by the surprising 'already' inaugurated by following Jesus" ("Discerning the Theopolitical," p. 332).

56. I note that Ben Quash also observes of Radical Orthodoxy that "there is very little attention given to particular, concrete, human realities" ("Radical Orthodoxy's Critique of Niebuhr," in *Reinhold Niebuhr and Contemporary Politics: God and Power,* ed. Richard Harries and Stephen Platten [Oxford: Oxford University Press, 2010], p. 69). Following Richard Roberts and Tim Jenkins, Quash locates the flaw in a neglect of "ethnography" — that is, "the effective representation and interpretation of what is actually happening in human lives" (Richard Roberts, "Theology and the Social Sciences," in *The Modern Theologians: An Introduction to Christian Theology since 1918,* 3rd ed., ed. David F. Ford with Rachel Muers [Oxford: Blackwell, 2005], p. 380; quoted in Quash, "Radical Orthodoxy's Critique of Niebuhr," p. 69).

willing to think again about who's inside and who's outside. We follow Jesus precisely in that we are open to discovering the presence of the Spirit among our own equivalents of sinners, tax collectors, and Gentiles.

If, however, the boundaries of God's kingdom extend beyond the walls of actual churches — if indeed the walls of some churches fall outside the boundaries of the kingdom — then the question arises: What is the point of actual, historical churches? And what sense should we make of faith in God outside of them?

In response to the second question, one famous option open to us, of course, is Karl Rahner's concept of anonymous Christianity.[57] This has been unpopular ever since postcolonial religious pluralists complained about its alleged paternalism. To call someone who does not confess God-in-Christ an "anonymous Christian," they say, is to measure her by an alien stick, to assimilate her to an ideal that is not her own, to ride roughshod over her *difference.* I have never been persuaded by this criticism. It seems to me that we have no choice but to evaluate things and people in terms of the truth as we see it, judging according to our own best lights. A Christian is bound to judge others — as he judges himself — in terms of Jesus Christ, as a Muslim is bound to judge in terms of Muhammad, and a Buddhist in terms of the Buddha. If someone were to call me "an anonymous Muslim," I would find in that no immediate cause for offense. But that is only because I do not assume that everything in Islamic theological, spiritual, and moral traditions is inimical to Christianity. If I did regard Islam as totally inimical, then I would welcome being called "an anonymous Muslim" about as much as I would welcome being called "an anonymous Nazi." Since I do not assume that Islam lacks *anything* that a Christian might find

57. See Karl Rahner, "Anonymous Christians," in *Theological Investigations VI: Concerning Vatican Council II,* trans. Karl-H. and Boniface Kruger (London: Darton, Longman, and Todd, 1969), pp. 390-98; "Atheism and Implicit Christianity," in *Theological Investigations IX: Writings of 1965-67, I,* trans. Graham Harrison (London: Darton, Longman, and Todd, 1972); "Anonymous Christianity and the Missionary Task of the Church," in *Theological Investigations XII: Confrontations 2,* trans. David Bourke (London: Darton, Longman, and Todd, 1974), pp. 161-78; "Observations on the Problem of the 'Anonymous Christian,'" in *Theological Investigations XIV: Ecclesiology, Questions in the Church, The Church in the World,* trans. David Bourke (London: Darton, Longman, and Todd, 1976), pp. 280-94.

commendable or admirable, I would not immediately resent the appellation. But I would want to inquire about the particular respects in which I am supposed to conform to *which version* of Islam. I would feel myself to be misrepresented, of course, if I were supposed to be a simple monotheist, while I am in fact a Trinitarian monotheist; and I would feel distinctly uneasy if I were being assimilated to Wahhabi Islam. But that might well not be what my Muslim interlocutor meant. What he did have in mind I could not presume to know a priori, but would need to find out.

To describe someone who does not confess God-in-Christ as nevertheless "an anonymous Christian" is to say that, from a Christian point of view, this non-Christian appears to be approximating the truth. It is to express a certain approval, and unless he utterly mistrusts the Christian issuing it, the non-Christian would have no reason to reject it out of hand. The description is certainly not one that he himself would give; but it might be true nonetheless. Sometimes others really do read us better than we read ourselves.

I do not think that the concept of "an anonymous Christian" is necessarily patronizing; but I do think that Barth's talk of "a virtual Christian" is preferable in certain respects.[58] This is true for two reasons. First, the word "virtual" recognizes the difference directly. It recognizes that the non-Christian has, for whatever reason, not yet *owned* Christian faith: he is almost but not quite Christian. It gives his lack of consent a certain room to breathe. Second, the word "virtual" puts the non-Christian on the same footing as the Christian. It recognizes that *both* of them fall short of perfection, that both are *in via*. The case is not that

---

58. See Karl Barth, *Church Dogmatics*, IV/4, *The Christian Life, Lecture Fragments,* trans. G. W. Bromiley (Edinburgh: T. & T. Clark, 1981), pp. 21-22. As I explained in *Hastening That Waits* (pp. 150-51), Barth's talk of the "virtuality" of non-Christians involves a stronger — and more dubious — claim than his talk of their "potentiality." To say that non-Christians are "potential" Christians is to say that they might yet be called by God-in-Christ and might yet respond affirmatively. But to claim them as "virtual" Christians is to say that they *have been reconciled* to God-in-Christ, but are not yet aware of it. In other words, Barth's "virtual" Christianity involves a soteriologically universalist claim, and it implies that the only difference between Christians and non-Christians is epistemic. I could not accompany Barth that far in 1993; nor do I do so now. What I approve of here are the logical implications of the word "virtual."

of the non-Christian measuring up to the Christian, but that of both of them (not yet) measuring up to Christ. According to properly *Christian* theology, that is the more accurate description.

But how can someone who does not confess that there is a God, or that God wears the face of Jesus, be claimed even as "a virtual Christian"? Failure to confess, of course, is not the same as hostility. It might simply betoken a certain lack of awareness or articulateness. Someone might live his life gladly, humbly, penitently, generously, resiliently, courageously, and hopefully *as if* the world were presided over by an intelligent, benevolent, radically compassionate, salvific, superhuman power, and yet not recognize what he takes for granted as tantamount to what theists call "God" and Christians call "God-in-Christ." But sometimes the failure to confess is quite deliberate. Sometimes it betokens not a mere lack of awareness but positive rejection. Even in such a case, however, it is possible that what is rejected is a misunderstood theism or Christianity. The rejection might be fueled by a particular experience — whether personal or social — in which "God" and "Christ" have come to connote something oppressive or dishonest. Or it might be motivated by genuine intellectual doubts about the coherence of theological theory.[59]

Rejection at one level, however, is compatible with acceptance at another. The human psyche, as we know, is not all of a piece. Sometimes what we confess with our lips we deny in our lives; and sometimes what we deny with our lips, we confess in our lives. There are avowed atheists and non-Christians who, despite their nonconfession, live as if there were a God who wears the face of Jesus.[60] If we are aware of our own in-

59. I have in mind here Albert Camus, who persisted in his practical commitment to humanism while frankly believing it to be theoretically absurd. I do not suppose that he wanted to find it so; he just did. The subtlety of these matters is well indicated by Camus's intriguing statement: "It's true that I don't believe in God, but that doesn't mean that I'm an atheist . . . ." (Olivier Todd, *Albert Camus: A Life,* trans. Benjamin Ivry [London: Vintage, 1998], p. 356).

60. The Second Vatican Council describes the saving faith of those outside the church in terms that sound (to my Protestant ears) moralistic: "Those who, through no fault of their own, do not know the Gospel of Christ or his Church, but who nevertheless seek God with a sincere heart, and, moved by his grace, try in their actions to do his will as they know it through the dictates of conscience — those too may achieve eternal salva-

ner inconsistencies, then we cannot take others' self-descriptions at face value or as the final word.

Confession and faith are not the same thing. Jesus himself said as much. But if genuine faith is possible in spite of the adamant contradiction of the biblical story, or in spite of mere ignorance of it, then what is the raison d'être of Christian churches? If genuine faith can be kindled by the Spirit apart from the proclamation of the gospel in the preaching, sacraments, and life of the churches, then what is the point of the proclamation? Why bother with it?

First of all, nonconfessional faith might well owe more to the churches' witness than first appears. Especially in the post-Christendom West, but also elsewhere in the wider, more or less Westernized world, the Christian story might in fact shape nonconfessors in ways to which they are largely oblivious.

Still, we may not suppose that God-in-Christ is incapable of communicating himself apart from the witness of Christian churches, be it direct or be it mediated by a Christianized culture. For if God were not able to communicate with individuals apart from those who confess him, then a confessing people would never have come about in the first place. Had God not been able to make himself known to Abraham in the pagan context of Ur of the Chaldees, then there would have been no Jewish people; and had he not been able to turn the ear of Jesus amidst first-century Palestinian Judaism, then there would have been no Christian church. The phenomenon of the religious or moral pioneer implies that the living God can manifest himself in more or less alien social environments. That, in turn, implies that the confession and witness of

---

tion" (*Lumen Gentium,* 16, in *Documents of Vatican II,* ed. Austin P. Flannery [Grand Rapids: Eerdmans, 1975], p. 367). While he invokes Vatican II in support of his notion of the "anonymous Christian" (e.g., "Anonymous Christians," p. 397; "Atheism and Implicit Christianity," passim), it is clear that Karl Rahner understands "implicit faith" to involve a tacit acknowledgment of God as the ground of an absolute moral demand, and a tacit acceptance of dependence on him (e.g., "Atheism and Implicit Christianity," pp. 153, 156, 159). However, if such faith is to be Christian and not merely theistic, it also needs to involve implicit trust in more-than-human forgiveness and implicit hope that things will come right in the end by the grace of more-than-human power. These may be betokened by a professed non-Christian's combination of self-critical humility, persistent moral commitment, and patient — even cheerful — resilience.

Christian churches is not essential or necessary for the communication of God-in-Christ, which is at once humbling (for ecclesial idealists) and reassuring (for ecclesial realists).

What is not essential or necessary or basic, however, might still be important. While Christian confessors and witnesses are bound always to *follow* the originating work of the Spirit, they might still make an important contribution to its confirmation and growth, both intellectually and practically. Perhaps there is a natural human drive to make explicit what is implicit, to articulate what is intuited, to confess in word and practice and institution one's innermost convictions.[61] If so, then the church's witness will help implicit Christianity find its proper voice. Moreover, the lack of theoretical confirmation must weaken the implicit Christian's practical commitments: the fact, for example, that Albert Camus viewed his own humanism as absurd surely cannot have *helped* his practical resolve. Accordingly, the church's telling a rational story that gives a cosmic home to the implicit Christian's practical commitments can only add to their strength. After all, whether an act is (held to be) right depends on whether its assumptions about the world are (held to be) true. Further, the implicit Christian will lack the benefit of the resources of intellectual and practical wisdom that identification with Christian tradition confers; this the church's witness can communicate. And further still, since the salvation of the world must eventually take *social* form, what is implicit and individual must become explicit and ecclesial.[62]

61. I take it that Rahner means something like this when he writes that "[t]he seed has no right to seek not to grow into a plant" ("Observations on the Problem of the 'Anonymous Christian,'" p. 291).

62. Rahner makes a similar point: "We are aware today in a quite new and inescapable way that man is a social being, a being who can exist only within such intercommunication with others throughout all of the dimension of human existence. And from this perspective we acquire a new understanding of Christian religion as an ecclesial religion" (*Foundations of the Christian Faith: An Introduction to the Idea of Christianity,* trans. William V. Dych [New York: Seabury, 1978], p. 323). This is a disappointingly rare exception to the rule that Rahner is better at asserting *that* implicit religion must or should become explicit than he is at explaining *why.* Eamonn Conway defends Rahner against the accusation that his concept of anonymous Christianity relativizes the church by showing that, for him, implicit Christianity is incomplete (*The Anonymous Christian — A Relativised Christianity? An Evaluation of Hans Urs von Balthasar's Criticisms of Karl Rahner's Theory of*

The fact that God-in-Christ can be somewhat known outside the walls of the Christian churches does not mean that the witness of those churches is redundant. It does mean that such witness is contingent on the saving initiative of the Holy Spirit. However, for those who are genuine believers and not Promethean wolves in sheep's clothing, creaturely contingency will merely deflate, not destabilize.

---

the *Anonymous Christian,* European University Studies, Series 23: Theology, vol. 485 [Frankfurt am Main: Peter Lang, 1993], pp. 134-38). What Conway leaves unclear — presumably because Rahner does not explain it — is *how* implicit Christian faith is deficient, and therefore *what* full creedal and ecclesial expression adds to it.

The Via Media: *A Barthian Thomism*

The Christian church is not redundant. It has a calling and a duty to tell the truth about God in the light of Jesus Christ, and about the human good and right action in the light of *this* God. The church's vocation holds, notwithstanding the fact that some who do not explicitly affirm God-in-Christ also grasp what is good and right, and even do so in a way that gestures at a given moral order, at hope for the lasting significance of human endeavor beyond the mortality of all things, and at the intelligibility of ultimate self-sacrifice for the sake of love and justice. After all, Christians believe that what they confess is *true* — and true not just for Christians. So why should they be surprised — even more, why should they feel threatened — that others also perceive moral reality, thanks to the order that is given in human nature and to the mundane presence of the Spirit of God-in-Christ? That their role is to follow the Spirit and confirm, maybe elaborate on, his original witness should satisfy. If it does not satisfy, then Christians risk reprising the role of the Prodigal Son's elder brother.

Since the truth that the church has to tell is of the God who loved the world in Jesus Christ, and since the good of that world is not only individual but also common, Christians should care to shape public life. Certainly, such life will sometimes be so corrupt that the only way to shape it for good is to replace it altogether, in which case Christians will answer their vocation by way of prophetic critique and alternative politics. At other times, however, public life will be morally ambiguous rather than irredeemably evil. And where public deliberation is properly secular, liberal, and polyglot, Christians should take the opportunity to say it as they see it, so loving the world as to orient it toward moral reality, and as to care not a fig about how distinctive their own identity appears. Impelled by their own theological convictions, Christians will recognize their non-Christian interlocutors to be not just sinners but *fellow* sinners, who may also be in the process of being drawn ever more closely to the one God who wears the face of Jesus. Accordingly, Christians will lay aside stereotypes and caricatures and resolve instead to find out what is actually there. They will approach others with a humble readiness to learn as well as to teach, and with an openness to discerning consensus, however fragmentary, provisional, and tense it may be. Keeping their evangelical talk from mere rhetoric, they will let its manner be disciplined by its content. Adopting humility, docility, patience, forbearance, forgiveness — as well as candid truthfulness — they will learn to love in conversation and thus to behave in public deliberation. And having learned, they may then teach.

I have sought neither narrativism nor autonomism, and neither secularism nor theological authoritarianism: instead, I have sought to plow a middle furrow between these two sets of options. Of course, middle ways tend to attract scorn. They tend to be seen as the resort of ditherers who cannot bring themselves to make a grown-up decision, or of wishful thinkers who fancy having their cake and still eating it. No doubt that is sometimes true; no doubt, what purports to be a third way is sometimes just a lazy, fanciful cobbling together of elements whose compatibility has not been wrought. But surely, this need not be so; surely, sometimes a third way can make up a stable *via media,* constructing the half-truths of unbalanced alternatives into a coherent synthesis. True, its colors may not flash as garishly. But since when was strength always stark? Surely, it can be subtle, too.

If the middle way set forth in this book needs a label to locate it in Christian theological tradition, then "Barthian Thomism" would serve well.[1] For "Thomism" is the substantive noun and "Barthian" the adjec-

---

1. The label "Barthian Thomism" serves well, but not perfectly. As historical systems of thought Barthianism and Thomism cannot be merged, for, while converging at some points, they are irreducibly opposed at others. "Barthian Thomism" therefore denotes a constructive integration, not of whole historical systems, but of certain characteristic elements.

tive, in order to signal that the created order comes logically before its narrative, christological qualification. What God the Son reveals about the human good itself can only be a confirmation or a development of what God the Father created in the first place. So far, so Thomist. However, some of what Jesus reveals about how we should act to defend and promote that good under the conditions of sin and in the light of eschatological hope is novel. In that sense, then, the christological narrative *changes* the natural law — or, to be precise, it changes what had wrongly or inadequately been understood to be the moral requirements of the principles of the human good lodged in unchanging human nature. So far, so Barthian.

Both Aquinas and Barth justify a Christian expectation that moral wisdom is to be found outside of the Christian church, that Christians might have something to learn from non-Christians, and that a measure of consensus between them is possible. But each reaches this position by a different route. Aquinas holds that natural reason has only been wounded and not destroyed by sin, whereas Barth holds that God-in-Christ is present to — and tacitly acknowledged by — "virtual Christians." Since I believe that there is only one God, the God who wears the face of Jesus, and that the acknowledgment of this God has always been important for right moral understanding, I do not recognize a "natural" moral reason that operates sufficiently apart from such faith. Nevertheless, I see no need to argue that human reason apart from faith is rendered entirely incapable of grasping any moral truth at all. I see no need to deny that it grasps moral fragments. What faithless reason lacks is a grasp of the true theological whole in which to order them. Furthermore, appearances can be deceiving. If the Spirit of God-in-Christ reveals himself beyond the walls of the church, then "faithless" reason will not always be so faithless after all. "Natural" moral reason will sometimes be less natural and more theologically informed than it confesses. All things considered, it seems to me that Barth's account of non-Christian moral insight is more theologically adequate, more subtle, and more generous than Aquinas's alternative.[2]

2. I do not doubt that there are Thomist interpretations of Aquinas that could — or do — spin him in a Barthian direction on this point. Nevertheless, it seems to me that the very concept of "natural" moral reason is problematic insofar as it denotes or connotes a natural faculty that is self-sufficient apart from "supernatural" revelation.

Barth's confidence in God's presence in the world is, of course, a correlate of his typically Protestant modesty regarding God's presence in the church. The church is not God — even practically speaking — nor is God the church's property. Nevertheless, modesty is not the same as diffidence. Thoroughly convinced of God's Christlike nature, Barth does not doubt that he is pleased to grace with his presence a church that is modest. It is precisely those who take seriously the godness of God, and therefore their own radical contingency, who are suitably disposed to receive him. Those who do not presume may be confident. This fine, ecclesiological line of Barth seems to me at once true to the spirit of Jesus and entirely salutary.

Barth's glad confidence in the sovereignty of God-in-Christ made him generously open to the world in principle, and moved him to authorize theological ethics to learn from nontheological disciplines and sources, albeit subject to Christocentric and theological criteria. In practice, however, his own ethics seldom did this and the ethical tradition that he has generated is not at all famous for it. By contrast, the Thomist tradition is famous for it, and from the very beginning its moral theology has been shaped by moral philosophy. It can be argued, of course, that in this shaping theology was more annexed than annexing. Be that as it may, the principle of the critical theological annexation of other realms of knowledge is absolutely correct and, notwithstanding the attendant dangers, it should be practiced.[3] It is ironic that, in taking Barth at his word here, one must pull him in a characteristically "Thomist" — rather than "Barthian" — direction.

At this point, my Barthian Thomism takes a typically British, Anglican turn. Among the mundane sources of knowledge that moral theology should be willing to learn from is concrete experience. Experience, of course, seldom comes pure; usually it is not simply given, but

3. I am aware that Barth's term "annexation" is too aggressive to capture the sense of fellowship that should characterize a Christian moral theologian's regard for his non-Christian interlocuter, who is also a creaturely sinner in need of — and perhaps tacitly responsive to — God's grace. Nor does it capture the reciprocity that should characterize their exchange. Nevertheless, "annexation" does have the merit of making clear that, notwithstanding quite proper give-and-take, Christian moral theology can only remain what it is by sticking to its basic theological guns and being *discriminating* in its giving and taking.

comprises both data and their interpretation. For that reason, one should not take it at face value but should approach it critically. Nevertheless, experience contains data that cannot be entirely dissolved into interpretation.[4] There is something *there,* of which an interpretation seeks to give an account, and in terms of which it is accountable. When the Christian ethicist seeks to make a judgment about what is going on in the world, then, she should take care to look before she thinks. Since the point of evangelical judging is to raise up the judged rather than puff up the judge, she will strive to do generous justice to the awkward particulars, bending her critical concepts accordingly.

This empirical bent has claim to be characteristically, perhaps distinctively Anglican on two grounds, one general and one particular. The general ground is that Anglican thought often shares in the typically British respect for the empirical. The particular ground is that the Anglican moralist Kenneth Kirk was (in 1927) the first person, as far as I am aware, to give considered expression to the insight that the experience of particular cases and their circumstances is not just the passive matter to which moral norms are applied, but may sometimes react against principles and rules to provoke their reformation.[5] That is, experience can be formative of moral reasoning: it can exercise a kind of legitimate moral authority. Barth, of course, would never have said such a thing. I have not noticed Aquinas saying it either; and, given the reassertion of ecclesiastical authority in post-Tridentine Roman Catholi-

---

4. For example, one's experience of the I.R.A.'s thirty-year-long campaign of violence in Northern Ireland's "Troubles" will vary according to whether one construes it in republican or unionist terms. Nevertheless, for example, republican readings have to reckon with the bare fact that republicans killed five times as many people as the British state's security forces did, and even killed more Roman Catholics. See Marie Smyth, "Putting the Past in its Place," in *Burying the Past: Making Peace and Doing Justice after Civil Conflict,* 2nd rev. ed., ed. Nigel Biggar (Washington, DC: Georgetown University Press, 2003), Tables 7.3 and 7.4, pp. 137-38.

5. K. E. Kirk, *Conscience and its Problems: An Introduction to Casuistry* (London: Longmans, Green, 1927), pp. 107-11. Kirk says that the process of moral knowledge "consists in the discovery, *modification,* and application of principles" (p. 111, italics added); and that "[t]he process of continuous revision, *amendment,* and extension of the Christian code," as given moral principles negotiate with significantly novel cases, is "an inevitable feature of the Church's life" (p. 108, italics added).

cism, it seems unlikely that Thomism between the 1560s and the 1950s would have said it.[6]

To look before one thinks and speaks is simply an expression of love. To speak in love is to speak with the intention of benefiting, and we cannot expect to benefit what we have not taken the trouble to understand. And in order to understand particular human beings in their concrete predicaments, it is not enough to hoist one's prejudices over them. An ethicist who is Christian should want to follow his Lord and Master in loving the world. And if he would love the world, he will play pastor before he plays prophet. For the only people a prophet has the right to prophesy against are those he has first cared to make his own.

---

6. In the wake of World War II, however, much Roman Catholic moral theology did begin to take seriously the historical dimension of moral life and thinking. See, e.g., James M. Gustafson, *Protestant and Roman Catholic Ethics: Prospects for Rapprochement* (Chicago: University of Chicago Press, 1978), pp. 46-59.

Bibliography

Aitken, Robin. *Can We Trust the BBC?* London: Continuum, 2007.

Andersen, Svend. "Die Rolle theologischer Argumentation in öffentlichen Leben." In *Religion und Theologie im öffentlichen Diskurs: Hermeneutische und ethische Perspektiven,* edited by Gotlind Ulshöfer. Arnoldshainer Texte, Bd. 132. Frankfurt am Main: Haag und Herchen Verlag, 2005.

Andersen, Svend, and Kees van Kooten Niekerk, eds. *Concern for the Other: Perspectives on the Ethics of K. E. Løgstrup.* Notre Dame, IN: University of Notre Dame Press, 2007.

Aquinas, Thomas. *Summa Theologiae.*

Ashworth, Jacinta, and Ian Farthing. *Churchgoing in the UK.* London: Tearfund, 2007.

Augustine. *City of God.*

Balthasar, Hans Urs von. *The Theology of Karl Barth.* Translated by Edward T. Oakes, SJ. San Francisco: Ignatius Press, 1992.

Barnes, Philip. "Was the Northern Ireland Conflict Religious?" *Journal of Contemporary Religion* 20, no. 1 (2005): 55-69.

Barth, Karl. *Against the Stream.* Edited by R. G. Smith. Translated by E. M. Delacour and Stanley Godman. London: SCM, 1954.

———. "The Christian Community and the Civil Community." In *Community, State, and Church: Three Essays.* Edited by Will Herberg. Translated by A. M. Hall, G. Ronald Howe, and Ronald Gregor Smith. Gloucester, MA: Peter Smith, 1968.

———. *Church Dogmatics.* Edited by G. W. Bromiley and T. F. Torrance. Vol. I, *The Doctrine of the Word of God,* part 1. Translated by G. W. Bromiley. Edinburgh: T. & T. Clark, 1975.

———. *Church Dogmatics.* Vol. II, *The Doctrine of God,* part 1. Translated by G. W. Bromiley et al. Edinburgh: T. & T. Clark, 1957.

———. *Church Dogmatics.* Vol. II, *The Doctrine of God,* part 2. Translated by J. C. Campbell et al. Edinburgh: T. & T. Clark, 1957.

———. *Church Dogmatics.* Vol. III, *The Doctrine of Creation,* part 2. Translated by Harold Knight et al. Edinburgh: T. & T. Clark, 1960.

———. *Church Dogmatics.* Vol. III, *The Doctrine of Creation,* part 4. Translated by A. T. MacKay et al. Edinburgh: T. & T. Clark, 1961.

———. *Church Dogmatics.* Vol. IV, *The Doctrine of Reconciliation,* part 1. Translated by G. W. Bromiley. Edinburgh: T. & T. Clark, 1956.

———. *Church Dogmatics.* Vol. IV, *The Doctrine of Reconciliation,* part 3.1. Translated by G. W. Bromiley. Edinburgh: T. & T. Clark, 1961.

———. *Church Dogmatics.* Vol. IV, *The Doctrine of Reconciliation,* part 3.2. Translated by G. W. Bromiley. Edinburgh: T. & T. Clark, 1961.

———. *The Christian Life. Church Dogmatics.* Vol. IV/4. *Lecture Fragments.* Translated by G. W. Bromiley. Grand Rapids: Eerdmans, 1981.

———. *The Holy Spirit and the Christian Life: The Theological Basis of Ethics.* Translated by R. Birch Hoyle. Louisville: Westminster John Knox, 1993.

———. *Karl Barth's Table Talk.* Edited by John D. Godsey. Scottish Journal of Theology Occasional Papers, no. 10. Edinburgh: Oliver and Boyd, 1963.

———. *A Letter to Great Britain from Switzerland.* Translated by E. H. Gordon. London: Sheldon Press, 1941.

Becker, Dieter. *Karl Barth und Martin Buber — Denker in dialogischer Nachbarschaft? Zur Bedeutung Martin Bubers für die Anthropologie Karl Barths.* Göttingen: Vanderhoeck und Rupprecht, 1986.

Biggar, Nigel. *Aiming to Kill: The Ethics of Suicide and Euthanasia.* London: Darton, Longman, and Todd, 2004.

———. "Any News of the Social Good?" *Theology* 91, no. 744 (November 1988): 493-98.

———. "A Case for Casuistry in the Church." *Modern Theology* 6, no. 1 (October 1989): 29-51.

———. "Forgiving Enemies in Ireland." *Journal of Religious Ethics* 36, no. 4 (December 2008): 559-79.

———. *The Hastening That Waits: Karl Barth's Ethics.* Oxford: Clarendon Press, 1993; 1995.

———. "Is Stanley Hauerwas Sectarian?" In *Faithfulness and Fortitude: In Conversation with the Theological Ethics of Stanley Hauerwas,* edited by Mark Thiessen Nation and Samuel Wells. Edinburgh: T. & T. Clark, 2000.

———. "Karl Barth and Germain Grisez: An Ecumenical *Rapprochement.*" In *The Revival of Natural Law: Philosophical, Theological, and Ethical Responses to the Finnis-Grisez School,* edited by Nigel Biggar and Rufus Black. Aldershot: Ashgate, 2000.

———. "Karl Barth's Ethics Revisited." In *Commanding Grace: Karl Barth's*

Theological Ethics, edited by Daniel Migliore. Grand Rapids: Eerdmans, 2010.

———. "Moral Reason in History: An Essay in Defence of Casuistry." In *Issues in Faith and History.* Scottish Bulletin of Evangelical Theology, Special Study 3. Edinburgh: Rutherford House, 1989.

———. "The New Testament and Violence: Round Two." *Studies in Christian Ethics* 23, no. 1 (2010): 73-80.

———. "Not Translation, but Conversation: Theology in Public Debate about Euthanasia." In *Religious Voices in Public Places,* edited by Nigel Biggar and Linda Hogan. Oxford: Oxford University Press, 2009.

———. "Saving the 'Secular': The Public Vocation of Moral Theology." *Journal of Religious Ethics* 37, no. 1 (March 2009): 159-78.

———. "Specify and Distinguish! Interpreting the New Testament on 'Non-violence.'" *Studies in Christian Ethics* 22, no. 2 (May 2009): 164-84.

———. *Theological Politics: A Critique of "Faith in the City," the Report of the Archbishop of Canterbury's Commission on Urban Priority Areas (1985).* Latimer Studies 29/30. Oxford: Latimer House, 1988.

———, ed. *Burying the Past: Making Peace and Doing Justice after Civil Conflict.* 2nd rev. ed. Washington, DC: Georgetown University Press, 2003.

———, ed. *Reckoning with Barth: Essays in Commemoration of the Centenary of Karl Barth's Birth.* Oxford: Mowbray, 1988.

———, and Linda Hogan, eds. *Religious Voices in Public Places.* Oxford: Oxford University Press, 2009.

Blair, Tony. "Faith and Globalisation." The Cardinal's Lectures 2008, Westminster Cathedral, London, April 3, 2008: http://tonyblairoffice.org/2008/04/speech-pn-faith-globalisation.html.

Brown, Callum. "'Best Not to Take it Too Far': How the British Cut Religion Down to Size": http://www.opendemocracy.net/globalization-aboutfaith/britain_religion_3335.jsp.

Butt, Hassan. "My Plea to Fellow Muslims: You Must Renounce Terror." *The Observer,* July 1, 2007.

Changing Britain. A Report of the Board of Social Responsibility of the General Synod of the Church of England. London: Church House Publishing, 1987.

Chapman, Mark D. *Doing God: Religion and Public Policy in Brown's Britain.* London: Darton, Longman, and Todd, 2008.

Church of England's Board for Social Responsibility. *The Church and the Bomb: Nuclear Weapons and the Christian Conscience.* A report of a working party under the chairmanship of the Bishop of Salisbury. London: Hodder and Stoughton, 1982.

Collins, Eamonn. *Killing Rage.* London: Granta, 1997.

Conway, Eamonn. *The Anonymous Christian — A Relativised Christianity? An Evaluation of Hans Urs von Balthasar's Criticisms of Karl Rahner's Theory of* the Anonymous Christian. European University Studies, Series 23: Theology, vol. 485. Frankfurt am Main: Peter Lang, 1993.

Curran, Charles, and Richard McCormick, SJ, eds. *The Distinctiveness of Christian Ethics.* Readings in Moral Theology, no. 2. New York: Paulist Press, 1980.

————, eds. *Natural Law and Theology.* Readings in Moral Theology, no. 7. New York: Paulist Press, 1991.

Davie, Grace. *Europe: The Exceptional Case; Parameters of Faith in the Modern World.* London: Darton, Longman, and Todd, 2002.

————. *Religion in Britain Since 1945: Believing without Belonging.* Oxford: Blackwell, 1994.

Eberle, Christopher. *Religious Conviction in Liberal Politics.* Cambridge: Cambridge University Press, 2002.

Faith in the City: A Call for Action by Church and Nation. A Report of the Archbishop of Canterbury's Commission on Urban Priority Areas. London: Church House Publishing, 1985.

Gregory, Eric. *Politics and the Order of Love: An Augustinian Ethic of Democratic Citizenship.* Chicago: University of Chicago Press, 2008.

Grisez, Germain. *The Way of the Lord Jesus.* 4 vols. Chicago: Franciscan Herald Press, 1983-93.

Gustafson, James. *Can Ethics Be Christian?* Chicago: University of Chicago Press, 1975.

————. *Protestant and Roman Catholic Ethics: Prospects for Rapprochement.* Chicago: University of Chicago Press, 1978.

Habermas, Jürgen. *The Future of Human Nature.* Translated by William Rehg, Max Pensky, and Hella Beister. Cambridge: Polity Press, 2003.

————. "Habermas entre démocratie et génétique." *Le Monde* 20 (Décembre 2002): 8.

————. *Zwischen Naturalismus und Religion: Philosophische Aufsätze.* Frankfurt am Main: Suhrkamp, 2005. English translation: *Between Naturalism and Religion: Philosophical Essays.* Cambridge: Polity Press, 2008.

Hand, Learned. "Mr. Justice Cardozo." *Harvard Law Review* 52 (1939): 362-63.

Hauerwas, Stanley. *Character and the Christian Life: A Study in Theological Ethics.* San Antonio: Trinity University Press, 1975.

————. *Dispatches from the Front: Theological Engagements with the Secular.* Durham: Duke University Press, 1994.

————. *The Hauerwas Reader.* Edited by John Berkman and Michael Cartwright. Durham: Duke University Press, 2001.

————. *The Peaceable Kingdom: A Primer in Christian Ethics.* Notre Dame, IN: Notre Dame University Press, 1983.

————. *Sanctify Them in the Truth: Holiness Exemplified.* Edinburgh: T. & T. Clark, 1998.

————. *Truthfulness and Tragedy: Further Explorations in Christian Ethics.* Notre Dame, IN: University of Notre Dame Press, 1977.

————. "Where Would I Be Without Friends?" In *Faithfulness and Fortitude: In Conversation with the Theological Ethics of Stanley Hauerwas,* edited by Mark Thiessen Nation and Sam Wells. Edinburgh: T. & T. Clark, 2000.

————. *With the Grain of the Universe: The Church's Witness and Natural Theology.* Grand Rapids: Brazos, 2001.

Hays, Richard. *The Moral Vision of the New Testament.* Edinburgh: T. & T. Clark, 1996.

————. "Narrate and Embody: A Response to Nigel Biggar." *Studies in Christian Ethics* 22, no. 2 (May 2009): 185-98.

Healy, Nicholas M. "Karl Barth's Ecclesiology Reconsidered." *Scottish Journal of Theology* 57, no. 3 (2004): 287-99.

Honecker, Martin. "Sterbehilfe und Euthanasie aus theologischer Sicht." In *Lebensverkürzung, Tötung und Serientötung — Eine interdisciplinäre Analyse der "Euthanasie,"* edited by Manfred Oehmichen. Lübeck: Schmidt-Römhild, 1996.

Hughes, Gerard, SJ. "The Authority of Christian Tradition and of Natural Law." In *Natural Law and Theology,* edited by Charles Curran and Richard McCormick, SJ. Readings in Moral Theology, no. 7. New York: Paulist Press, 1991.

Husain, Ed. *The Islamist.* London: Penguin, 2007.

Hütter, Reinhard. "The Church as Public: Dogma, Practice, and the Holy Spirit." *Pro Ecclesia* (Summer 1994): 334-61.

Insole, Christopher. "Discerning the Theopolitical: A Response to Cavanaugh's Reimagining of Political Space." *Political Theology* 7, no. 3 (2006): 323-35.

Junker-Kenny, Maureen. "Between Postsecular Society and the Neutral State: Religion as a Resource for Public Reason." In *Religious Voices in Public Places,* edited by Nigel Biggar and Linda Hogan. Oxford: Oxford University Press, 2009.

Kirk, K. E. *Conscience and its Problems: An Introduction to Casuistry.* London: Longmans, Green, 1927.

Lehmann, Paul. *Ethics in a Christian Context.* New York: Harper and Row, 1963.

Lloyd, John. *What the Media Are Doing to Our Politics.* London: Constable and Robinson, 2004.

Løgstrup, Knud Ejler. *Beyond the Ethical Demand.* Edited and with introduction by Kees van Kooten Niekerk. Translated by Susan Dew, Heidi Flegal, and George Pattison. Notre Dame, IN: University of Notre Dame Press, 2007.

————. *The Ethical Demand.* Introduction by Hans Fink and Alasdair MacIntyre. Translated by Theodor I. Jensen, Gary Puckering, and Eric Watson. Notre Dame, IN: University of Notre Dame Press, 1997.

MacNamara, Vincent. *Faith and Ethics: Recent Roman Catholicism.* Dublin: Gill and MacMillan, 1985.

Maher, Shiraz. "How I Escaped Islamism." *The Sunday Times,* August 12, 2007.

Markus, R. A. *Christianity and the Secular.* Notre Dame, IN: University of Notre Dame Press, 2006.

————. *Saeculum: History and Society in the Theology of St Augustine.* Cambridge: Cambridge University Press, 1970.

Martin, David. *Does Christianity Cause War?* Oxford: Oxford University Press, 1997.

Mauriac, François. *Bloc-notes.* 5 vols. Edited by Jean Touzot. Vol. 1, "1952-57." Paris: Seuil, 1993.

McCormick, Richard, SJ. "Does Religious Faith Add to Ethical Perception?" In *The Distinctiveness of Christian Ethics,* edited by Charles Curran and Richard McCormick, SJ. Readings in Moral Theology, no. 2. New York: Paulist Press, 1980.

McNeill, John T. "Natural Law in the Teaching of the Reformers." *Journal of Religion* 26 (1946): 168-82.

Melanchthon, Philipp. *Epitome philosophiae moralis.* 1541.

Methuen, Charlotte. *Science and Theology in the Reformation: Studies in Theological Interpretation and Astronomical Observation in Sixteenth-Century Germany.* Edinburgh: T. & T. Clark, 2008.

Milbank, John. *Being Reconciled: Ontology and Pardon.* London: Routledge, 2003.

————. "Enclaves, or Where is the Church?" *New Blackfriars* 73, no. 861 (June 1992): 341-52.

————. "The Gift of Ruling: Secularization and Political Authority." *New Blackfriars* 85, no. 996 (March 2004): 212-38.

————. *Theology and Social Theory: Beyond Secular Reason.* Oxford: Blackwell, 1990.

————. *The Word Made Strange: Theology, Language, Culture.* Oxford: Blackwell, 1997.

Nation, Mark Thiessen, and Sam Wells, eds. *Faithfulness and Fortitude: In Conversation with the Theological Ethics of Stanley Hauerwas.* Edinburgh: T. & T. Clark, 2000.

Nawaz, Maajid. "Why I Joined the British jihad — and Why I Rejected It." *The Sunday Times,* September 16, 2007, News Review, p. 8.

Niebuhr, Reinhold. *The Children of Light and the Children of Darkness.* London: Nisbet, 1945.

————. *Christian Realism and Political Problems.* London: Faber and Faber, 1953.

————. *Essays in Applied Christianity.* Edited by D. B. Robertson. New York: Living Age Books, 1959.

————. *Faith and History: A Comparison of Christian and Modern Views of History.* New York: Charles Scribner's Sons, 1949.

————. *An Interpretation of Christian Ethics.* New York: Seabury Press, 1979.

————. *Moral Man and Immoral Society: A Study in Ethics and Politics.* New York: Charles Scribner's Sons, 1960.

————. *The Nature and Destiny of Man: A Christian Interpretation.* 2 vols. New York: Charles Scribner's Sons, 1964.

O'Callaghan, Sean. *The Informer.* London: BCA, 1998.

O'Donovan, Oliver. *The Desire of the Nations: Rediscovering the Roots of Political Theology.* Cambridge: Cambridge University Press, 1996.

————. *The Just War Revisited.* Cambridge: Cambridge University Press, 2003.

————. *The Ways of Judgment.* The 2003 Bampton Lectures. Grand Rapids: Eerdmans, 2005.

Park, Alison, et al., eds. *British Social Attitudes: The 26th Report.* London: Sage, 2010.

Porter, Jean. "Is the Embryo a Person? Arguing with the Catholic Traditions." *Commonweal,* February 8, 2002, pp. 8-13.

————. *Natural and Divine Law.* Notre Dame, IN: Notre Dame University Press, 1999.

Preston, Ronald. "Appendix 2: Middle Axioms in Christian Social Ethics." In *Church and Society in the Late Twentieth Century: The Economic and Political Task.* London: SCM, 1983.

Quash, Ben. "Radical Orthodoxy's Critique of Niebuhr." In *Reinhold Niebuhr and Contemporary Politics: God and Power,* edited by Richard Harries and Stephen Platten. Oxford: Oxford University Press, 2010.

Rahner, Karl. "Anonymous Christianity and the Missionary Task of the Church." In *Theological Investigations XII: Confrontations 2.* Translated by David Bourke. London: Darton, Longman, and Todd, 1974.

————. "Anonymous Christians." In *Theological Investigations VI: Concerning Vatican Council II.* Translated by Karl-H. and Boniface Kruger. London: Darton, Longman, and Todd, 1969.

————. "Atheism and Implicit Christianity." In *Theological Investigations IX: Writings of 1965-67, I.* Translated by Graham Harrison. London: Darton, Longman, and Todd, 1972.

————. *Foundations of the Christian Faith: An Introduction to the Idea of Christianity.* Translated by William V. Dych. New York: Seabury, 1978.

————. "Observations on the Problem of the 'Anonymous Christian.'" In *Theological Investigations XIV: Ecclesiology, Questions in the Church, the Church in the World.* Translated by David Bourke. London: Darton, Longman, and Todd, 1976.

Ramsey, Paul. "The Case of the Curious Exception." In *Norm and Context in*

Christian Ethics, edited by Gene Outka and Paul Ramsey. New York: Scribner's, 1968.

Rawls, John. *The Law of Peoples*. Cambridge, MA: Harvard University Press, 1999.

Rhees, Rush, ed. *Ludwig Wittgenstein: Personal Recollections*. Oxford: Blackwell, 1981.

Robbins, Keith. *England, Ireland, Scotland, Wales: The Christian Church, 1900-2000*. The Oxford History of the Christian Church. Oxford: Oxford University Press, 2008.

Roberts, Richard. "Theology and the Social Sciences." In *The Modern Theologians: An Introduction to Christian Theology since 1918*, edited by David F. Ford and Rachel Muers. 3rd ed. Oxford: Blackwell, 2005.

Schüller, Bruno, SJ. "A Contribution to the Theological Discussion of Natural Law." In *Natural Law and Theology*, edited by Charles Curran and Richard McCormick, SJ. Readings in Moral Theology, no. 7. New York: Paulist Press, 1991.

—————. "The Debate on the Specific Character of Christian Ethics: Some Remarks." In *The Distinctiveness of Christian Ethics*, edited by Charles Curran and Richard McCormick, SJ. Readings in Moral Theology, no. 2. New York: Paulist Press, 1980.

Second Vatican Council. *Lumen Gentium*. In *Documents of Vatican II*, edited by Austin P. Flannery. Grand Rapids: Eerdmans, 1975.

Smyth, Marie. "Putting the Past in its Place." In *Burying the Past: Making Peace and Doing Justice after Civil Conflict*, edited by Nigel Biggar. 2nd ed. Washington, DC: Georgetown University Press, 2003.

Temple, William. *Christianity and the Social Order*. New York: Penguin, 1942.

Todd, Olivier. *Albert Camus: A Life*. Translated by Benjamin Ivry. London: Vintage, 1998.

United Kingdom Government. Census, April 2001: www.statistics.gov.uk/cci/nugget.asp?id+293.

Webster, John. *Barth's Ethics of Reconciliation*. Cambridge: Cambridge University Press, 1995.

Williams, Rowan. "Archbishop's Presidential Address." General Synod of the Church of England, February 10, 2009: www.archbishopofcanterbury.org/2169.

Wilson, Peter H. *Europe's Tragedy: A History of the Thirty Years War*. London: Allen Lane, 2009.

Wittgenstein, Ludwig. *Philosophical Investigations*. Translated by G. E. M. Anscombe. Oxford: Blackwell, 1972.

Wright, Tom. *Who Was Jesus?* London: SPCK, 1992.

Index

Abortion, 43

Abstraction, 13-16, 17-18, 23; *and* stereotyping, 95-96, 98-99, 108

Analogy, 13, 14, 15-16, 18, 23

Andersen, Svend, 32-34, 35-36

Anglican Christian socialism, 5

Anglican Communion, 76-77

Anglicanism, 110-11

Anthropology, 3, 4, 6, 84-85, 87

Aquinas, Thomas, 29, 30, 37, 64, 108-10. *See also* Thomism

Argument, theologico-ethical, Chapter 4

Aristotle, 81, 92

Augustine, 42-43, 46, 61, 97-98

Authority, appeal to, 67-71

Autonomy, ethical, 31-38

"Autonomy ethics," 36-38

Balthasar, Hans Urs von, 83

Barnes, Philip, 63n.1

Barth, Karl, xvi, 2, 6, 7, 12, 16, 18, 19-20, 30, 65, 68, 80, 82-87, 89, 90-95, 101-2, 108-10, 111; and "annexation," 20, 110; and "potential" Christianity, 85-88; and "theological" and "Christian" eth-ics, 20-22; and "virtual" Christian-ity, 101-3, 109

"Barthian Thomism," Conclusion

Becker, Dieter, 85n.12

Blair, Tony, 16, 56-57

Bland, Tony, 12

Bible
Genesis 1, 18
Genesis 1:26-28, 64
Wisdom literature, 27
Ecclesiastes, 64
Matthew 7:21-23, 27
Matthew 13:24-30, 27
Luke 12:33, 14
Luke 23:34, 28, 81
Luke 24:13-35, 47n.6
Sermon on the Mount, 64
Johannine literature, 81
John 20:11-18, 47n.6
Romans 13, 64
Romans 13:1-4, 16
1 Corinthians 15:35-57, 48n.6
Ephesians 4:26, 16
1 John 4:20, 26n.2
Pastoral Epistles, 27
Revelation 3:20, 85
and Public discourse, 65-68. *See also* Interpretation, biblical

121